the METROPOLITAN BAKERY COOKBOOK

the
METROPOLITAN BAKERY
COOKBOOK

Artisan Breads, Pastries, *and* Desserts

from Philadelphia's Premier Bakery

JAMES BARRETT *and* WENDY SMITH BORN

Photographs by Catherine Hennessy

RODALE

Printed in the United States of America
Rodale Inc. makes every effort to use acid-free ∞, recycled paper ♻.

Photographs on pages v, 6, 38, 56, 79, 98, 124, 139, 191, 194, 202, and 225 by Peggy Galson; all others by Catherine Hennessy
Book design by Christina Gaugler

Library of Congress Cataloging-in-Publication Data

Barrett, James, date.
    The Metropolitan Bakery cookbook : artisan breads, pastries, and desserts from Philadelphia's premier bakery / James Barrett and Wendy Smith Born ; photographs by Catherine Hennessy.
        p.   cm.
    Includes index.
    ISBN 1–57954–759–1 hardcover
    1. Baking.   I. Born, Wendy Smith, date.   II. Title.
TX763.B357   2003
641.8'15—dc21   2003014003

Distributed to the book trade by St. Martin's Press

2 4 6 8 10 9 7 5 3 1 hardcover

WE INSPIRE AND ENABLE PEOPLE TO IMPROVE
THEIR LIVES AND THE WORLD AROUND THEM

FOR MORE OF OUR PRODUCTS
WWW.RODALESTORE.COM
(800) 848-4735

To James and Lorraine Barrett for supporting James through the years
and to his Grandma Tucci, who ignited his passion for food at an early age.

—J. A. B.

To Chris, Ian, Galen, and Kyley Born, who have endured 10 years
of benign neglect as we built Metropolitan.

—W. S. B.

To our customers, our associates, and our friends, who have all inspired us
to sustain Metropolitan Bakery over these first 10 years.

CONTENTS

FOREWORD

This book is written by two people who have been an important part of our lives over the past two decades—as dear friends, as integral players in the founding of our own company, and as business leaders in Philadelphia. Wendy Born was there the day we opened the White Dog Café 20 years ago, and did everything from waitressing to sandwich-making in the fledgling start-up. James Barrett began 15 years ago as pastry chef and bread baker extraordinaire, and to this day guests still enjoy his acclaimed breads and milk chocolate cream pie.

When Wendy and James first started Metropolitan Bakery, we were their first and only customers. Now they are known nationwide for producing artisanal bread and pastries using only the finest ingredients. The very best restaurants in the Philadelphia region have Metropolitan Bakery breads for their guests, and thousands of customers frequent the Metropolitan Bakery shops to savor the irresistible multitude of freshly baked treats, hard-to-find cheeses, delicious toppings and salads, and the best coffee anywhere.

But James and Wendy are more than great bakers and good business-people: They strive with integrity and passion to make a difference in the lives of the bakery staff and the customers they serve. They are always thinking of ways to please people and provide a caring environment for tasting and shopping. This book is another way for James and Wendy to share and inspire their readers with a little more of what makes Metropolitan Bakery the most special place in town.

Judy Wicks and Kevin von Klause
White Dog Café

April 2003

ACKNOWLEDGMENTS

First and foremost, we wish to thank all of the people who keep Metropolitan Bakery going 363 days a year, as well as all of our past associates who helped to launch and shape Metropolitan Bakery into what it is today: Sue Gracia, who has been a critical part of our entire operation; Donn Garten, the backbone of our retail business; Ilon Silverman, Jerry Franks, and the night crew who have baked thousands of loaves of bread every single night of the year while Carlos Berrios and the day production crew have mixed and shaped those loaves day in and day out. Thanks to our retail managers, Jason, Barb, Lexi, and Nicki, who have run our stores and nurtured our customers.

Thanks also to all the talented people who have worked on this book. Our recipe testers labored for endless hours on mathematical calculations and baking to get the recipes right: Barbara Bonnet, Carlos and Edwin (Mango) Berrios, Andrew Fuerste-Henry, Stacy Galasso, Patti Parkis, Ivette Molina, and Karen Lauer. Our recipe tasters have tried and boldly critiqued the finished product: Chris, Ian, Galen, and Kyley Born; Theresa Wallen; and the associates of Metropolitan Bakery and 1900 Rittenhouse Square. Lisa Ekus, our agent, suggested to us years ago that we write this book and kept at us until we actually agreed. She has supported us throughout the project. Thanks to the many people at Rodale who have helped us produce the book: Anne Egan, our original editor, who first saw the potential; Margot Schupf, our editor, who encouraged us and energized us to meet our deadlines and finish the book; and Chris Gaugler, our thoughtful and capable designer for the book. Catherine Hennessy shot beautiful photographs, often on a moment's notice. Peggy Galson's exquisite photographs captured our early days, and Jennifer Hansen, our designer, resurfaced just in time to lend her expertise to this project. Carol Prager, our extraordinary recipe editor, tweaked and refined our recipes. Sarah Gracia patiently deciphered our handwriting and typed much of the manuscript. Thanks to Beth D'Addono for helping us craft the original proposal.

Finally, thanks to Judy Wicks and Kevin von Klause at the White Dog Café, who were our very first customers and who have remained our trusted friends through these years.

INTRODUCTION

On a cloudy, cold day in November 1993, we opened the doors to Metropolitan Bakery. For all intents and purposes, we were ready for business, but our opening was anything but "grand." A few weeks before, the local newspaper had kindly written a piece on our soon-to-be bakery. Incredibly, we hadn't even sold a loaf and already people seemed excited and were eagerly awaiting this "new" old-world bread they had read about.

Unfortunately for us, the piece incorrectly stated our opening as being two weeks earlier than we had planned. The store was far from complete, still very much a construction site, and would certainly not be the bakery we had hoped for by this new date. Nonetheless, we were faced with the choice of either opening early or disappointing our future customers. The choice was simple. The bread would be ready, and everything else would have to fall into place. So, that day, we waited until the afternoon after the construction workers had left, stocked a baker's rack with freshly baked bread, and, with a shoebox as our cash register, opened Metropolitan Bakery to a line that stretched down the sidewalk.

That unexpected early opening and our scramble to somehow make things work was a lesson that continues to instruct us even now, ten years later, five stores bigger, and more than one hundred wholesale accounts larger. The bread is the boss, and it is the bread that directs our course and sustains our customers to this day.

Many years before Metropolitan Bakery, James and I became friends while I was managing partner and he was pastry chef at the White Dog Café. Our mutual love of food and especially bread, combined with a similar spirit and drive, quickly forged a strong friendship. Experimental, innovative, and socially conscious, the White Dog was a young restaurant where the creation of great, honest food was primary. Frustrated with the lack of character and taste in the restaurant's yeasted baguettes and rolls, James searched for a way to create the types of breads he had savored in his Italian grandmother's kitchen when he was young. The breads he sought were those not meant to be an afterthought on the dinner table, but meant to complement and enhance the meal with their hearty crusts, chewy interiors, and complex flavors. Influenced by the burgeoning artisan bread movement on the West Coast, James found the key to the bread he envisioned was the use of natural yeasts created from the simple, yet delicate, combination of flour, water, and fermenting grapes. Unlike commercial yeasts, these "starters" enhanced the quality and taste of the bread, rather than diluting it.

Unfortunately, it was not quite as easy as he had hoped, and his first experiments resulted in less-than-stunning results. Eventually, though, the breads became richer in flavor and consistency, which only served to intensify our interest in artisan baking. Soon, that passion guided us to Europe and the West Coast to learn more; as we did, the vision for our own bakery grew stronger and stronger.

Once we were back in Philadelphia, Metropolitan Bakery was a clear and real concept. At least, it was to us. As we sought financing with a solid business plan and fifteen years combined food experience, others could not see our wonderful bakery quite as clearly as we did. No one would give us a cent. Undeterred, we put a sizable amount of our own money and an even greater amount of faith into turning the dream of our bakery into a reality.

Money, it turned out, was to be the easy part, as the early days of the bakery tested our determination and endurance to simply keep Metropolitan functioning. Often, James slept on a table at the bakery for days at a time, leaving only for a shower and a change of clothes. I began my days at 4 A.M. at the production bakery, filling orders and delivering bread to the few wholesale customers we had. A few hours later, at 7:30 A.M., I would open the store and stay there until close. Both of us would catch a couple hours of sleep and begin all over again the next day. The list of challenges since those days has been huge and, for good and bad, continues to grow. Over the years, we've experienced power outages and equipment breakdowns. We've had to bake bread at local restaurants when our ovens weren't functioning. Through it all, we have kept our wits and kept the bread baking.

Rather than dim our spirit, the challenges of the bakery only serve to invigorate and sustain our original vision. The challenges are secondary to the rewards we have received from the hard work and dedication it has taken to get us where we are today and where we hope to be tomorrow. These rewards come from taking someone who has never baked before and watching them develop and grow. The rewards come from giving our associates the opportunity to become proficient at a trade and to create a livelihood that will support them and their families. And finally, the rewards—which we hope you will discover within the recipes of this book—come from creating great, honest food that is a delight to eat and share with others.

October 2003

BREADS

We believe that naturally leavened bread has a personality all its own. It is defined by its ingredients, by the climate and environment in which it is made, and by the people who make it. Naturally leavened breads are characterized by intense, lingering, earthy flavors; by a chewy, resilient texture; and by a thick, crackling crust. In this chapter, we explain starters and why it is worthwhile to go through the trouble of making them. Starters add immeasurably to the texture, taste, and natural fermentation process of memorable breads. Our no-nonsense explanations will demystify the process, which isn't so much hard as it is time consuming. We'll walk you through the bread-baking process, explaining each step along the way. We know that not everybody is going to attempt to bake bread at home, but we encourage you to try it, at least once.

Natural Starters

A natural starter is the building block of a bread recipe. It is neither as complex nor as mysterious as one might think. The principles are easy to understand. Flour is mixed with water. In a warm, moist environment, the wild yeast and microorganisms in the air and on the flour will feed on the sugar in the flour and multiply. To ensure success in capturing a wild yeast culture, most bakers will use a catalyst such as mashed bananas, apples, raisins, or the skins of Concord grapes.

Once you have initialized a natural culture, known as a chef, it is important to keep it healthy and active. This is achieved by giving the starter feedings or refreshments. This has a dual purpose: It replenishes the exhausted food supply for the wild yeasts, and it keeps the acid/alkaline balance of the starter in check. A healthy starter culture will appear bubbly and have a pleasant sour aroma. In contrast, a neglected starter culture will appear flat and have a strong, offensive aroma. The loaves produced with a healthy natural starter will have a crust that is a rich, burnished, mahogany tone. The interior will be an irregular network of translucent webs of gluten. The aroma will resemble that of fresh cheese: slightly sour, pungent, and nutty like a toasted grain. Natural starters will extend the shelf life of breads, acting as a natural preservative.

Once the 6-day process of capturing the wild yeast has been accomplished, the culture must be strengthened and sustained. To achieve this, 3 refreshments are given to the culture. Most home bakers do not make bread on a daily basis, but a starter may be kept alive by slowing down its activity in the refrigerator or by making it dormant in the freezer. If kept in the freezer, the starter will need to be thawed completely and then be activated with its 3 refreshments. If refrigerated, the starter should be brought to room temperature until it shows signs of activity (bubbling on the surface). Each time you plan to use your starter to leaven a bread dough, it must go through the 3-refreshment process

Starters can replace the commercial yeast in bread recipes. The average substitution is 20 percent to 30 percent of the total flour weight. For example, if your recipe calls for 4 cups of flour, you will need approximately ¾ cup to 1¼ cup of the active starter. It is necessary to adjust the water amount accordingly, to achieve the correct consistency for the bread dough.

The Chef

Day One

  1 cup bread flour

  ½ cup water (72°F)

  1 tablespoon organic apple juice

In a large glass bowl, combine the flour, water, and apple juice. Whisk vigorously to incorporate air into the mixture and to ensure that there are no lumps. Cover the bowl tightly with plastic wrap and let the mixture ferment at room temperature for 3 days. On the third day, the mixture (chef) should appear to be alive: bubbly and spongy. This indicates a successful capturing of the wild yeasts. (If there is no activity then, however, you will need to begin the process again.) Next, it is necessary to strengthen the yeast culture.

Day Three

  1 cup bread flour

  ½ cup water (68°F)

Skim off the dry surface of the chef and discard. Discard half the remaining chef. You should have approximately half of the chef left. Transfer the reserved chef to a clean bowl. Add the flour and water. Whisk vigorously until smooth. Cover the bowl tightly with plastic wrap and let the chef ferment at room temperature 1 day.

Day Four

  1 cup bread flour

  ½ cup water (68°F)

Check to see that the chef has doubled in size and appears spongy. Repeat process as directed for Day Three.

Day Five

  1 cup bread flour

  ½ cup water (68°F)

Check to see that the chef has doubled in size and appears spongy. Repeat process as directed for Day Three.

Day Six

Check to see that the chef has doubled in size and appears spongy. By this point, you should have successfully captured and strengthened a culture of wild yeast. This "ripe" chef can be used to initialize all of the following starters, which in turn may be used to leaven the breads in this chapter. After measuring the amount of the chef you'll need for a recipe, discard any of the remaining chef or use it to prepare another recipe.

White Starter

⅔ cup ripe Chef (page 8)

½ cup water (68°F)

⅓ cup bread flour

In a large glass bowl, whisk together the chef and water until the chef dissolves and the mixture becomes wet and sticky. Whisk in the flour until the mixture becomes smooth. Cover the bowl tightly with plastic wrap and let the mixture ferment at room temperature 6 hours or until bubbly. Then refrigerate the starter overnight or up to 14 hours.

Day Two (Second Refreshment)

1 cup water (68°F)

¾ cup bread flour

Check to see that the starter has doubled in size then collapsed slightly. Add the water and flour to the starter; whisk until smooth. Cover the bowl tightly with plastic wrap and let the starter ferment at room temperature 6 hours, until bubbly. Then refrigerate the starter overnight.

Day Three (Third Refreshment)

2 cups water (74°F)

1½ cups bread flour

Check to see that the starter has doubled in size then collapsed slightly. Add the water and flour to the starter; whisk until the flour is incorporated. Cover the bowl tightly with plastic wrap. Then refrigerate the starter overnight.

Day Four

The starter is now ready to properly leaven the bread recipe of your choice. It should appear bubbly and slightly spongy and have a bright, sour aroma. This is referred to as an "active" starter. Before using the active starter, let it come to room temperature, about 2 hours. After measuring the amount of starter you'll need for a recipe, set aside ¾ cup, discarding any of the remaining starter. Refrigerate the reserved starter up to 2 weeks or freeze up to 3 months. Before you use the reserved starter in a recipe, return it to room temperature (thawing it in the refrigerator overnight, if frozen). Repeat the 3-step refreshment process, starting with Day One (the ¾ cup reserved starter will now replace the chef).

Whole Wheat Starter

While the White Starter is a pourable consistency, this starter is mixed to a firm consistency to slow down its fermentation process.

Day One (First Refreshment)

½ cup ripe Chef (page 8)

½ cup whole wheat flour

¼ cup water (68°F)

In a large glass bowl with a wooden spoon, stir together the chef, flour, and water until the dough is firm and smooth. Cover the bowl tightly with plastic wrap and let the mixture ferment at room temperature 6 hours or until bubbly. Then refrigerate the starter overnight.

Day Two (Second Refreshment)

1 cup whole wheat flour

½ cup water (68°F)

Check to see that the starter has doubled in size. With a wooden spoon, stir in the flour and water. Cover the bowl tightly with plastic wrap and let the starter ferment at room temperature 6 hours or until bubbly. Then refrigerate the starter overnight.

Day Three (Third Refreshment)

2 cups whole wheat flour

1 cup water (68°F)

Check to see that the starter has doubled in size. With a wooden spoon, stir in the flour and water. Cover the bowl tightly with plastic wrap and let the starter ferment at room temperature 6 hours or until bubbly. Then refrigerate the starter overnight.

Day Four

This "active" starter is now ready to use. It should appear bubbly and slightly spongy and have a bright, sour aroma. Before using, let the starter come to room temperature, about 2 hours. After measuring the amount of starter you'll need for a recipe, set aside ¾ cup, discarding any of the remaining starter. Refrigerate the reserved starter up to 2 weeks or freeze up to 3 months. Before you use the reserved starter in a recipe, return it to room temperature (thawing it in the refrigerator overnight, if frozen). Repeat the 3-step refreshment process, starting with Day One (the ¾ cup reserved starter will now replace the chef).

Rye Starter

Day One (First Refreshment)

½ cup ripe Chef (page 8)

½ cup dark rye flour

¼ cup water (68°F)

In a large glass bowl with a wooden spoon, stir together the chef, flour, and water until a smooth, thick paste is formed. Cover the bowl tightly with plastic wrap and let the mixture ferment at room temperature 4 hours or until bubbly. Then refrigerate the starter overnight.

Day Two (Second Refreshment)

1 cup dark rye flour

½ cup water (68°F)

Check to see that the starter has doubled in size. With a wooden spoon, stir in the flour and water. Cover the bowl tightly with plastic wrap and let the mixture ferment at room temperature 4 hours or until bubbly. Then refrigerate the starter overnight.

Day Three (Third Refreshment)

2 cups dark rye flour

1½ cups water (68°F)

Check to see that the starter has doubled in size. With a whisk, stir in the flour and water. Cover the bowl tightly with plastic wrap and let the mixture ferment at room temperature 4 hours or until bubbly. Then refrigerate the starter overnight.

Day Four

This "active" starter is now ready to use. It should appear bubbly and slightly spongy and have a bright, sour aroma. Before using, let the starter come to room temperature, about 2 hours. After measuring the amount of starter you'll need for a recipe, set aside ½ cup, discarding any of the remaining starter. Refrigerate the reserved starter up to 2 weeks or freeze up to 3 months. Before you use the reserved starter in a recipe, return it to room temperature (thawing it in the refrigerator overnight, if frozen). Repeat the 3-step refreshment process, starting with Day One (the ½ cup reserved starter will now replace the chef).

Whole Wheat Levain

A levain is a 3-step refreshment process that begins with a ripe starter. During each refreshment, fresh water and enough bread flour are added to develop a soft dough. Levain lends great flavor and texture to our Caramelized Onion–Thyme Bread (page 26) and Whole Grain Sandwich Bread (page 24).

Day One (First Refreshment)

- ⅓ cup active Whole Wheat Starter (page 10)
- 3 tablespoons water (70°F)
- ½ cup bread flour
- 1 tablespoon plus 1 teaspoon whole wheat flour

In a large bowl with a wooden spoon, stir together the starter and water. Add the bread flour and whole wheat flour; stir until a soft dough is formed. Cover the bowl tightly with plastic wrap and let the mixture ferment at room temperature 12 hours, until doubled in size.

Day Two (Second Refreshment)

- ¾ cup water (70°F)
- 1 cup plus 2 tablespoons bread flour
- ½ cup whole wheat flour

Check to see that the levain has doubled in size then collapsed slightly. In the bowl of a heavy-duty mixer with a dough hook attachment, dissolve the First Refreshment in the water at low speed. Add the bread flour and whole wheat flour; mix until a soft dough is formed. Mix the dough 2 minutes. Transfer the dough to a lightly oiled bowl; cover the bowl tightly with plastic wrap. Let the dough stand at room temperature 4 hours until active but not doubled in size. Then refrigerate the dough overnight.

Day Three (Third Refreshment)

1½ cups water (70°F)

2⅓ cups bread flour

1 cup plus 1 tablespoon whole wheat flour

Check to see that the Second Refreshment has doubled in size then collapsed slightly; transfer to the bowl of a heavy-duty mixer. With a dough hook attachment at low speed, dissolve the Second Refreshment in the water. Add the bread flour and whole wheat flour. Mix until a soft dough is formed. Mix the dough 3 minutes or until smooth and slightly elastic. Return the dough to the oiled bowl; cover the bowl tightly with plastic wrap. Let the dough stand at room temperature 4 hours until it begins to rise. Then refrigerate the dough overnight.

Day Four

The levain is now ready to use. It should have doubled in size. Before using, let the levain come to room temperature, 1 to 2 hours. After measuring the amount of levain you'll need for a recipe, set aside ⅓ cup, discarding any of the remaining levain. Refrigerate the reserved levain up to 2 weeks or freeze up to 3 months. Before you use the reserved levain in a recipe, return it to room temperature (thawing it in the refrigerator overnight, if frozen). Repeat the 3-step refreshment process, starting with Day One (the ⅓ cup reserved levain will now replace the whole wheat starter).

COUNTRY BREAD

This is one of our favorite breads, pure and simple in flavor with just a hint of nuttiness from the natural grains. Don't be afraid to bake this bread to a deep golden brown—the darker the loaf, the more the sugars in the crust are caramelized and the better the flavor.

Preferment

- ⅓ cup active Whole Wheat Starter (page 10)
- 1 cup plus 1 tablespoon water (68°F)
- 1½ cups bread flour

Dough

- 1 cup water (74°F)
- 1 teaspoon malt extract (see Resources, page 238)
- 3 cups bread flour, plus extra flour for preparation
- 1 tablespoon fine sea salt
- Yellow cornmeal, for preparation

Preferment

1. In a large bowl, dissolve the starter in the water. With a wooden spoon, stir in the flour until a pancake-like batter is formed. Cover the bowl tightly with plastic wrap; let ferment at room temperature 8 hours (or up to 12 hours).

Dough

2. With a rubber spatula, scrape the preferment into the bowl of a heavy-duty mixer; add ¾ cup of the water, the malt extract, and flour. With a dough hook attachment at low speed, mix until the dough forms a shaggy mass, about 4 minutes. Sprinkle the salt over the dough. Let the dough rest 15 minutes.

3. At low speed, mix the salt into the dough for 2 minutes. Increase the speed to medium. Knead the dough 8 minutes, gradually add the remaining ¼ cup water, 2 tablespoons at a time, until thoroughly incorporated after each addition. Test for proper gluten development (see "Testing Gluten Development," page 17). The dough should be smooth and elastic and pull away from the sides of the bowl. The temperature

should be 78° to 80°F when tested with an instant-read thermometer. Transfer the dough to a lightly oiled bowl or container at least twice its size and cover tightly with plastic wrap. Let rise in a cool, draft-free place until doubled in size, 4 to 5 hours.

4. Generously coat a cloth-lined proofing basket (banneton) (see Resources, page 238) with sifted flour, or line a small open basket with a towel and flour it. Set aside.

5. Turn the dough out onto a lightly floured surface and flatten to a disk with the palms of your hands. Turning the disk counterclockwise, pick up the edges and fold over to the center until a complete revolution has been made. Repeat this process one more time, so that the size of the disk is half of what it was and a rough ball is formed. Turn the ball seam-side down. Cup the ball with both hands and round the dough until the ball is compact and firm. Seal the bottom of the ball where the creases converge; turn the ball seam-side up; transfer to the prepared basket. Cover the basket tightly with plastic wrap and let the dough rise at room temperature 1 hour. Transfer the basket to the refrigerator; refrigerate the dough to rise slowly overnight or up to 12 hours.

6. Remove the dough from the refrigerator; let come to room temperature, up to 2 hours.

7. Meanwhile, at least 20 minutes before baking, place a large baking stone on the center oven rack. Preheat the oven to 500°F.

8. Sprinkle a baker's peel or the back of a baking sheet with cornmeal. Carefully invert the dough onto the peel; remove the basket. With a lame (see Equipment, page 241) or a sharp knife, score the top of the loaf in a decorative pattern. (See "Scoring Your Loaves," page 17.) Working quickly, open the oven door and generously spray the entire oven cavity with water (taking care not to spray the oven lightbulb) to create steam. (See "Creating Steam in Your Oven," page 17.) Slide the loaf onto the baking stone and close the oven door. Reduce the oven temperature to 425°F. Bake 3 minutes. Open the oven door and spray all around the loaf. Close the oven door. Bake 3 minutes. Repeat spraying the oven walls. Bake 40 to 50 minutes, until the loaf is dark golden and sounds hollow when tapped on the bottom. Transfer the loaf to a wire rack and cool completely.

Makes 1 large loaf

BAKING TIPS

Here's how to test for gluten development (or the dough's extendability).

1. Tear off a small piece of kneaded dough. With lightly floured hands, very gently stretch and turn the dough (as if you were shaping a pizza crust) until it becomes sheer enough to see through. The dough should stretch evenly without tearing. If it tears before it is sheer, continue kneading 2 to 3 minutes to develop the gluten then test again.

2. Insert an instant-read thermometer into the dough. Wait a few seconds to register the temperature. If the dough does not register 78° to 80°F, return the dough to the mixer and knead 1 minute more.

Creating Steam in Your Oven

Baking loaves with steam during the first part of baking helps to soften the exterior crust. This allows for optimum loaf expansion during the final activity of the yeast before it expires. It also gelatinizes the surface of the loaf, creating a shiny finish.

If you don't have a spray bottle to create steam, place a baking pan at least 2 inches deep on the floor of your oven. Preheat the pan along with the baking stone at least 20 minutes before baking. Just before placing the loaf in the oven, very carefully pour lukewarm water into the pan.

Scoring Your Loaves

Scoring a loaf is the baker's signature. The scoring allows the loaf to expand without bursting wildly in the oven and lends a decorative appearance to the loaf. Scoring works best using a 3-inch lame to which you attach a double-edge razor blade. Alternatively, a sharp serrated knife may be used.

POTATO-ROSEMARY BREAD

This bread is a meal unto itself. Most potato bread recipes call for boiling the potatoes to be used in the dough. We prefer to bake them so as not to dilute their flavor. The potatoes, rosemary, and olive oil are a classic marriage, and the potatoes give the final bread a wonderful moistness.

1½ pounds Russet potatoes

1 cup water (68°F)

¾ cup active White Starter (page 9)

4¼ cups bread flour, plus extra flour for preparation

2 tablespoons whole wheat flour

¼ cup extra-virgin olive oil

1 tablespoon coarsely chopped fresh rosemary

1 tablespoon fine sea salt

Yellow cornmeal, for preparation

1. Preheat the oven to 400°F. Place the potatoes on a baking tray. Bake until the potatoes are tender when tested with a small, sharp knife, 50 to 60 minutes. Cool completely. Peel the skins and discard.

2. In the bowl of a heavy-duty mixer, combine the potatoes, water, and starter. With a dough hook attachment at low speed, mix until the potatoes are lightly broken up, about 2 minutes. Stop the mixer. Add bread flour, whole wheat flour, oil, and rosemary. At low speed, mix until a firm, but moist, dough is formed, about 4 minutes. Sprinkle the salt over the dough. Let the dough rest 15 minutes.

3. At low speed, mix the salt into the dough, 2 minutes. Increase the speed to medium. Knead the dough 8 minutes. Test for proper gluten development (see "Testing Gluten Development," page 17). The dough should be smooth and elastic and pull away from the sides of the bowl. The temperature should be 78° to 80°F when tested with an instant-read thermometer. Transfer the dough to a lightly oiled bowl or container at least twice its size, and cover tightly with plastic wrap. Let rise in a cool, draft-free place until doubled in size, 4 to 5 hours.

4. Generously coat 2 cloth-lined proofing baskets (bannetons) (see Resources, page 238) with sifted flour, or line 2 medium open baskets with a towel and flour them. Set both aside.

5. Turn the dough out onto a lightly floured surface. Divide the dough into 2 equal pieces. Shape each into a round loaf. Turn each loaf seam-side up; transfer to the prepared baskets. Cover the baskets tightly with plastic wrap. Refrigerate to rise slowly overnight or up to 12 hours.

6. Remove the loaves from the refrigerator; let come to room temperature, about 1 hour.

7. Meanwhile, at least 20 minutes before baking, place a large baking stone on the center oven rack. Preheat the oven to 450°F. (Note: If the baking stone is not large enough to accommodate both loaves, reserve 1 loaf in the refrigerator until ready to bake.)

8. Sprinkle a baker's peel or the back of a baking sheet with cornmeal. Carefully invert 1 loaf onto the peel; remove the basket. With a lame (see Equipment, page 241) or a sharp knife, lightly score the surface of the loaf in a crisscross pattern (see "Scoring Your Loaves," page 17). If your stone is large enough to accommodate both loaves, invert the second loaf onto the peel and score the top. Working quickly, open the oven door and generously spray the entire oven cavity with water (taking care not to spray the oven lightbulb) to create steam. (See "Creating Steam in Your Oven," page 17.) Slide the loaf (or loaves) onto the baking stone. Close the oven door. Bake 3 minutes. Open the oven door and spray all around the loaf. Close the oven door. Bake 3 minutes. Repeat spraying the oven walls. Bake 40 minutes, until the loaf is dark brown and sounds hollow when tapped on the bottom. Transfer the loaf to a wire rack and cool completely. (Repeat, baking the remaining loaf, if necessary.)

Makes 2 loaves

FRENCH BERRY ROLLS

James developed this roll in response to our customers' requests for low-fat muffins. Our French berry roll is a wholesome small bread, bursting with sun-dried berries and flavored with malt extract and wheat germ.

½ cup (3 ounces) sun-dried strawberries (see Resources, page 238)

½ cup (2½ ounces) dried blueberries (see Resources, page 238)

½ cup (2½ ounces) dried tart cherries (see Resources, page 238)

½ cup (2 ounces) dried cranberries (see Resources, page 238)

¾ cup active White Starter (page 9)

1 cup plus 1 tablespoon water (70°F)

4½ cups bread flour, plus extra flour for preparation

3 tablespoons malt extract (see Resources, page 238)

1 tablespoon fine sea salt

1 tablespoon wheat germ

Yellow cornmeal, for preparation

1. In a large bowl, combine berries and enough warm water to cover. Soak 10 minutes; drain well. Set aside.

2. In the bowl of a heavy-duty mixer, combine the starter, water, flour, and malt extract. With a dough hook attachment at low speed, mix until the dough forms a shaggy mass, 4 minutes. Sprinkle the salt and wheat germ over the dough. Let the dough rest 15 minutes.

3. At low speed, mix the salt and wheat germ into the dough for 2 minutes. Increase the speed to medium. Knead the dough 8 minutes. Test for proper gluten development (see "Testing Gluten Development," page 17). The dough should be smooth and elastic and pull away from the sides of the bowl. The temperature should be 78° to 80°F when tested with an instant-read thermometer. Reduce the speed to low and stir the softened berries into the dough. Transfer the dough to a lightly oiled bowl or container at least twice its size, and cover tightly with plastic wrap. Let rise at room temperature until doubled in size, 4 to 6 hours.

4. Turn the dough out on a lightly floured work surface; divide into 12 equal pieces. Shape each piece into a round ball, then fold in half. Use the palm of your hand to seal the seam closed. Roll each piece back and forth into an oval with exaggerated pointed ends.

5. Line a large baking tray with clean tea towels. Lightly coat the towels with sifted flour. Place each roll, seam-side up and about 1" apart, on the prepared towels. Gently pull up the towel between each roll to form a pleat 1½" to 2" higher than the tops of the rolls. Cover the rolls with a damp towel or plastic wrap; refrigerate to rise slowly overnight or up to 12 hours.

6. Preheat the oven to 475°F. Sprinkle a large baking sheet with cornmeal.

7. Carefully transfer the rolls, seam-side down, to the prepared sheet. With a lame (see Equipment, page 241) or a sharp knife, cut 1 shallow diagonal slash lengthwise down the center of each roll. Working quickly, open the oven door and generously spray the entire oven cavity with water (taking care not to spray the oven lightbulb) to create steam. (See "Creating Steam in Your Oven," page 17.) Place the sheet of rolls on the center oven rack. Close the oven door. Bake 3 minutes. Repeat spraying the oven walls. Close the oven door. Reduce the oven temperature to 400°F. Bake 15 minutes, until the rolls are deep golden brown. Transfer the rolls to a wire rack and cool completely.

Makes 12 rolls

PAN SOBAO

In bakeries and markets throughout Puerto Rico, it is common to find these long, plump, shiny loaves. Carlos Berrios, our daytime production manager, was born and raised in Puerto Rico. He developed this version of pan sobao *to incorporate Metropolitan's bread-making techniques.*

Sponge

 3/4 cup active White Starter (page 9)

 1/2 cup water (72°F)

 1 cup bread flour

Dough

 1 teaspoon active dry yeast

 1 tablespoon granulated sugar

 3/4 cup water

 3 cups bread flour, plus extra flour for preparation

 4 tablespoons lard or unsalted butter

 1 tablespoon fine sea salt

 Yellow cornmeal, for preparation

Sponge

1. In a large bowl with a wooden spoon, stir together the starter, water, and flour until it forms a very soft dough. Cover the bowl tightly with plastic wrap and let the sponge rise at room temperature until doubled in size, 6 to 8 hours.

Dough

2. In the bowl of a heavy-duty electric mixer, combine the sponge, yeast, sugar, and water. With a dough hook attachment at low speed, mix until the sponge is dissolved. Add the flour and lard. Mix until the dough forms a shaggy mass, about 3 minutes. Sprinkle the salt over the dough. Let the dough rest 15 minutes.

3. At low speed, mix the salt into the dough for 2 minutes. Increase the speed to medium. Knead the dough 8 to 10 minutes. Test for proper gluten development (see "Testing Gluten Development," page 17). The dough should be smooth and elastic and pull away from the sides of the bowl. The temperature should be 78° to 80°F when tested with an instant-read thermometer. Transfer the dough to a lightly oiled bowl or

container at least twice its size, and cover tightly with plastic wrap. Let rise at room temperature until doubled in size, about 3 hours.

4. Turn the dough out onto a lightly floured surface; divide into 2 equal pieces. Flatten 1 piece of dough into a rectangle, with 1 long side facing you. Fold the top edge down to the center of the rectangle. Fold the bottom edge up to meet in the center. Starting from the top left edge, fold the top down to meet the opposite edge and close the loaf. Starting from the left, use the palm of your hand to seal the seam closed. Shape the dough into a 12" loaf, rolling the dough back and forth from the center to the edges, exerting extra pressure on the edges to taper the ends.

5. Line a large baking tray with clean tea towels; lightly coat the towels with sifted flour. Place the loaf, seam-side up, on the prepared towels. Repeat shaping the remaining piece of dough; place seam-side up and 2" apart from the first loaf. Gently pull up the towel between the loaves to form a pleat 2" higher than the tops of the loaves. Cover the loaves with damp tea towels or plastic wrap and let rise at room temperature until doubled in size, about 2 hours.

6. Meanwhile, at least 20 minutes before baking, place a large baking stone on the center oven rack. Preheat the oven to 450°F. (Note: If the baking stone is not large enough to accommodate both loaves, reserve 1 loaf in the refrigerator until ready to bake.)

7. Sprinkle a baker's peel (see Resources, page 238) or the back of a baking sheet with cornmeal. Pull the edges of the towel to separate the risen loaves. Carefully roll 1 loaf off the towel and place, seam-side down, on the prepared peel. With a lame (see Equipment, page 241) or a sharp knife, cut 3 shallow diagonal slashes, slightly overlapping, lengthwise down the center of the loaf. (If your stone is large enough to accommodate both loaves, roll the second loaf over onto the peel and score the surface; see "Scoring Your Loaves," page 17.) Working quickly, open the oven door and generously spray the entire oven cavity with water (taking care not to spray the oven lightbulb) to create steam. (See "Creating Steam in Your Oven," page 17.) Slide the loaf (or loaves) onto the baking stone. Close the oven door. Bake 3 minutes. Open the oven door and spray all around the loaf. Close the oven door. Bake 3 minutes. Repeat. Bake 35 minutes, until the loaf is golden brown and sounds hollow when tapped on the bottom. Transfer the loaf to a wire rack and cool completely.

Makes 2 loaves

WHOLE GRAIN SANDWICH BREAD

The grains in this bread are toasted so their natural flavor is highly pronounced. The addition of yeast to this whole wheat levain bread helps to lighten the texture, making it adaptable to both sandwiches and toast.

1¾ cups active Whole Wheat Levain (page 12)

1¾ cups water (72°F)

1 teaspoon active dry yeast

2½ cups bread flour, plus extra flour for preparation

1¼ cups whole wheat flour

1¼ cups (8 ounces) Toasted Grain Mix

2 tablespoons molasses

2 tablespoons honey

2 tablespoons grits

2 tablespoons cracked wheat

2½ teaspoons fine sea salt

1. In the bowl of a heavy-duty mixer, combine the levain, water, and yeast. With a dough hook attachment at low speed, mix to dissolve the levain and the yeast. Add the bread flour, whole wheat flour, grain mix, molasses, honey, grits, and cracked wheat. Mix until the dough forms a shaggy mass, about 3 minutes. Sprinkle the salt over the dough. Let the dough rest 20 minutes.

2. At low speed, mix the salt into the dough for 2 minutes. Increase the speed to medium; knead the dough 8 to 10 minutes. Test for proper gluten development (see "Testing Gluten Development," page 17). The dough should be smooth and elastic, but wet to the touch. The temperature should be 78° to 80°F when tested with an instant-read thermometer. Transfer the dough to a lightly oiled bowl or container at least twice its size and cover tightly with plastic wrap. Let rise in a cool, draft-free place until doubled in size, about 2 hours.

3. Lightly brush the bottoms and sides of two 8½" × 4½" loaf pans with safflower oil (or use 2 nonstick loaf pans). Set aside.

4. Turn the dough out onto a lightly floured surface; divide into 2 equal pieces. Flatten 1 piece of dough into a 5" × 7" rectangle, with 1 short side facing you. Starting from a short side, roll up the length of the dough, pinching the crease with each rotation. Starting from the left, use the palm of your hand to seal the seam closed. Gently roll

the cylinder back and forth until it is even; do not taper the ends. Place the loaf, seam-side down, in a prepared pan (the ends of the loaf should reach the ends of the pan). Repeat the process with the remaining dough.

5. Place the loaf pans on a large baking tray. Cover the pans loosely with plastic wrap. Let rise at room temperature until doubled in size, about 2 hours. (Or refrigerate the loaves to rise slowly overnight or up to 10 hours. The next day, let the loaves come to room temperature to finish rising, approximately 1 hour.)

6. Preheat the oven to 400°F. Working quickly, open the oven door and generously spray the entire oven cavity with water (taking care not to spray the oven lightbulb) to create steam. (See "Creating Steam in Your Oven," page 17.) Uncover the loaves and arrange the baking tray on the center oven rack. Close the oven door. Bake 3 minutes. Open the oven door and spray all around the loaves. Close the oven door. Bake 3 minutes. Repeat spraying the oven walls. Close the oven door. Bake 35 to 40 minutes, until loaves are dark golden brown. (To test for doneness, remove 1 loaf from a pan. It should sound hollow when tapped on the bottom.) Cool the loaves in the pans on a wire rack 5 minutes. Remove the loaves from the pans and cool completely on the wire rack. (If the loaves are left in the pans to cool, they will become soggy.)

Makes 2 loaves

TOASTED GRAIN MIX

¼ cup sesame seeds

¼ cup millet

¼ cup flax seeds

¼ cup sunflower seeds, shelled

¼ cup pumpkin seeds, shelled

¼ cup old-fashioned oats

1. Preheat the oven to 350°F.

2. In a bowl, combine the grains and the seeds. Spread the mixture in an even layer on a baking tray. Bake on the center oven rack 12 to 15 minutes, until toasted and golden brown. Cool.

Makes 1½ cups

CARAMELIZED ONION–THYME BREAD

This is one of the earliest breads in our repertoire. The richness and the sweetness of the caramelized onions, the addition of the aromatic fresh thyme, and the dark, crispy crust satisfy all of the senses at once.

1½ cups active Whole Wheat Levain (page 12)

1¼ cups water (72°F)

1 teaspoon malt extract (see Resources, page 238)

3 cups plus 2½ tablespoons bread flour, plus extra flour for preparation

2 tablespoons chopped fresh thyme, plus extra for sprinkling

1 tablespoon fine sea salt

1 cup Caramelized Onions (page 28)

1. In the bowl of a heavy-duty mixer, combine the levain, water, malt extract, flour, and the 2 tablespoons thyme. With a dough hook attachment at low speed, mix until the dough forms a shaggy mass, about 2 minutes. Sprinkle the salt over the dough. Let the dough rest 15 minutes.

2. At low speed, mix the salt into the dough for 1 minute. Increase the speed to medium. Knead the dough 8 to 10 minutes. Test for proper gluten development (see "Testing Gluten Development," page 17). The dough should be smooth and elastic and pull away from the sides of the bowl. The temperature should be 78° to 80°F when tested with an instant-read thermometer. Transfer the dough to a lightly oiled bowl or container at least twice its size, and cover tightly with plastic wrap. Let rise at room temperature until doubled in size, about 4 hours.

3. Turn the dough out onto a lightly floured surface. Use your fingertips to dimple the dough and spread it into a 12" × 16" rectangle with 1 long side facing you. Spread the caramelized onions over the dough. Sprinkle the remaining thyme over the onions. Fold the bottom third of the dough, letter style, up to the center of the rectangle. Fold the remaining dough over the top to meet the opposite edge. Fold the left-hand edge over to the center. Fold the right-hand edge over to the opposite side to form a 6" × 9" package. Turn the package over and press lightly to seal. Cover the package loosely with a tea towel and let rest 15 minutes.

4. Line 2 baking trays with parchment paper. Sift an even layer of flour over the paper. Set aside.

5. Uncover the package. With a bench knife or sharp knife, cut the package into two 6" × 4½" pieces. Transfer 1 piece, cut-side down, to each prepared tray. (Each piece should be standing on a very narrow side with a strip of onion filling directly facing the parchment paper.) Gently stretch each piece to elongate and shape into an oval loaf. Cover each loaf with a damp tea towel or plastic wrap, and let rise at room temperature until doubled in size, 2 hours.

6. Uncover the loaves; gently stretch each loaf so it becomes longer and wider. (Do not deflate the loaves.) Cover the loaves with damp towels or plastic wrap and let rest 30 minutes.

7. Meanwhile, place a large baking stone on the center oven rack. Preheat the oven to 450°F.

8. Uncover 1 loaf and place a piece of parchment paper over the top. (Note: If the baking stone is not large enough to accommodate both loaves, reserve 1 loaf in the refrigerator until ready to bake.) Gripping both ends of the sheet of parchment paper covering the loaf and with your thumbs underneath the tray, carefully flip the loaf over onto a baker's peel so that the loaf is cut-side up and the onion filling is exposed. Remove the top sheet of parchment paper. (If your stone is large enough to accommodate both loaves, cover the remaining loaf with another piece of parchment and invert as directed.) Working quickly, open the oven door and generously spray the entire oven cavity with water (taking care not to spray the oven lightbulb) to create steam. (See "Creating Steam in Your Oven," page 17.) Leaving the loaf (or loaves) on the parchment paper, slide it on to the baking stone. Close the oven door. Bake 3 minutes. Open the oven door and spray all around the loaf. Close the oven door. Bake 3 minutes. Repeat spraying the oven walls. Close the oven door. Reduce the oven temperature to 425°F. Bake 35 to 40 minutes, until dark golden brown and loaf sounds hollow when tapped on the bottom. Transfer the loaf to a wire rack and cool completely. (Repeat, baking the remaining loaf, if necessary.)

Makes 2 loaves

CARAMELIZED ONIONS

4   pounds (about 6) Spanish onions

½   cup extra-virgin olive oil

1   tablespoon granulated sugar

2   teaspoons kosher salt

¼   teaspoon freshly ground black pepper

½   teaspoon balsamic or sherry vinegar

1. Cut the root and stem off the onions; discard. Slice the onions in half and peel away the outer 2 layers. Cut onions into ¼"-thick slices.

2. In a saucepot, combine the onions, oil, sugar, salt, and pepper. Cook over medium heat, stirring, until the onions soften, about 2 minutes. Cover the pot, reduce the heat to medium-low, and cook the onions 20 minutes, stirring occasionally to prevent scorching. (If the heat seems too high, reduce it slightly.) Uncover and continue to cook until the juices reduce and the onions caramelize, 15 to 20 minutes more. Remove the pot from the heat; stir in the vinegar. Cool the onions, then refrigerate in an airtight container for up to 2 weeks.

Makes 3 ½ cups

APPLE-RYE BREAD

Rye flours are tricky to deal with, so many bakers shy away from them. We maintain a separate rye starter to leaven our rye breads because we feel it adds incomparable flavor.

---

1 ½ cups active Rye Starter (page 11)

2 cups water (70°F)

2 teaspoons malt extract (see Resources, page 238)

2 tablespoons hard apple cider

4 ½ cups bread flour, plus extra flour for preparation

¾ cup dark rye flour

1 tablespoon fine sea salt

2 large Granny Smith apples, peeled, cored, and halved

2 tablespoons honey

Yellow cornmeal, for preparation

1. In the bowl of a heavy-duty mixer, combine the rye starter, water, malt extract, and cider. With a dough hook attachment at low speed, mix until the starter is dissolved. Add the bread flour and rye flour; mix until the dough forms a shaggy mass. Sprinkle the salt over the dough. Let the dough rest 15 minutes.

2. At low speed, mix the salt into the dough for 2 minutes. Increase the speed to medium-low. Knead the dough 10 minutes. Test for proper gluten development (see "Testing Gluten Development," page 17). The dough should pull away from the sides of the bowl but still feel slightly tacky and sticky. Transfer the dough to a lightly oiled bowl or container at least twice its size, and cover tightly with plastic wrap. Let the dough rise at room temperature 2 hours.

3. Meanwhile, preheat the oven to 400°F. Cut each apple half into 8 slices. Spread the slices on a baking tray; drizzle with the honey. Bake the apples 8 minutes (they should still be firm). Cool completely.

4. Turn the dough out onto a lightly floured surface. Flatten the dough into a rectangle, with 1 long side facing you. Spread the apples over the surface. Fold the top third of the dough down to the center of the rectangle. Fold the bottom third of the dough to meet the top edge of the rectangle on the opposite side. Fold the left-hand edge of the

dough to the center of the rectangle. Fold the right-hand edge to the center so that the edges meet. Pinch the edges to seal. Return the dough, seam-side down, to the same oiled bowl. Cover the bowl tightly with plastic wrap and let the dough rise 2 hours.

5. Generously coat 2 cloth-lined oval proofing baskets (bannetons) (see Resources, page 238) with sifted flour or line 2 medium open oval baskets with towels and flour them. Set aside.

6. Turn the dough out onto a lightly floured surface; divide into 2 equal pieces. Using additional flour as needed (rye breads tend to be slightly sticky), flatten 1 piece of the dough into a rectangle, with 1 long side facing you. Fold the top third of the dough down to the center of the rectangle. Fold the bottom third up to the center so that the edges meet. Fold the left-hand edge of the dough to the center of the rectangle. Fold the right-hand edge to the center so that the edges meet. Pinch the edges to seal. With both hands over the surface, gently roll the dough into an even cylinder; pinch edges under. Transfer the loaf to a prepared basket. Repeat the process with the remaining dough. Cover the baskets loosely with plastic wrap. Refrigerate the baskets so that the loaves rise slowly, 6 to 8 hours.

7. Meanwhile, at least 20 minutes before baking, place a large baking stone on the center oven rack. Preheat the oven to 500°F. (Note: If the baking stone is not large enough to accommodate both loaves, reserve 1 loaf in the refrigerator until ready to bake.)

8. Sprinkle a baker's peel (see Resources, page 238) or the back of a baking sheet with the cornmeal. Carefully invert 1 loaf onto the peel; remove the basket. With a lame (see Equipment, page 241) or a sharp knife, cut 5 shallow slashes across the center of the loaf. (If your stone is large enough to accommodate both loaves, invert the second loaf onto the peel and score the top; see "Scoring Your Loaves," page 17.) Working quickly, open the oven door and generously spray the entire oven cavity with water (taking care not to spray the oven lightbulb) to create steam. (See "Creating Steam in Your Oven," page 17.) Slide the loaf (or loaves) onto the baking stone. Close the oven door. Reduce the oven temperature to 450°F. Bake 3 minutes. Open the oven door and spray all around the loaf. Close the oven door. Bake 3 minutes. Repeat spraying the oven walls. Close the oven door. Bake about 45 minutes, until the loaf is dark mahogany brown and sounds hollow when tapped on the bottom. Transfer the loaf to a wire rack and cool completely. (Repeat, baking the remaining loaf, if necessary.)

Makes 2 loaves

FRENCH BAGUETTE

Our baguette uses a preferment, which helps to create a crisper, crunchy crust with a moist interior and an irregular crumb. The small amount of yeast and the longer fermentation impart a decisively nutty flavor.

Preferment

1 teaspoon active dry yeast

¾ cup lukewarm water (80°F)

1½ cups all-purpose flour

¼ teaspoon fine sea salt

Dough

2½ cups all-purpose flour, plus extra flour for preparation

1¼ cups water

1¼ teaspoons fine sea salt

Yellow cornmeal, for preparation

Preferment

1. In a large bowl, dissolve the yeast in the water. Stir in the flour and salt until a soft dough is formed. Cover and refrigerate 12 hours.

2. Remove the preferment from the refrigerator. Let it stand until at room temperature, 1 hour.

Dough

3. In the bowl of a heavy-duty mixer, combine the preferment, flour, and water. With a dough hook attachment at low speed, mix until the dough forms a shaggy mass, about 4 minutes. Sprinkle the salt over the dough. Let the dough rest 15 minutes.

4. At low speed, mix the salt into the dough. Increase the speed to medium. Knead the dough 8 to 10 minutes. Test for proper gluten development (see "Testing Gluten Development," page 17). The dough should be smooth and elastic and pull away from the sides of the mixing bowl.

5. Lightly oil a large bowl; transfer the dough to the prepared bowl. Cover the bowl with plastic wrap and let the dough rise in a cool, draft-free place, 1 hour. Fold the dough down to deflate. Cover the bowl and let the dough rise until doubled in size, about 1 hour.

6. Turn the dough out onto a lightly floured surface; divide into 3 equal pieces. Flatten 1 piece of dough into a rectangle, with 1 long side facing you. Fold the bottom third of the dough, letter style, up to the center of the rectangle. Fold the remaining dough over the top to meet the opposite edge. Starting from the left, use the palm of your hand to seal the seam. Gently roll the baguette back and forth into an 18"-long log, tapering the ends. Repeat with the remaining 2 pieces of dough.

7. Line a large baking tray with clean tea towels. Sprinkle the towels lightly with flour. Arrange the baguettes, seam-side up and about 1" apart, on the prepared towels. Gently pull up the towel between each baguette to form a pleat 1½" to 2" higher than the tops of the baguettes. Cover the baguettes with damp tea towels and let rise in a cool place until doubled in size, about 2 hours.

8. Meanwhile, at least 20 minutes before baking, place a large baking stone on the center oven rack. Preheat the oven to 450°F.

9. Sprinkle a baker's peel with cornmeal. Carefully transfer 1 baguette, seam-side down, to the prepared peel. With a lame (see Equipment, page 241) or a sharp knife, cut 3 shallow diagonal slashes, slightly overlapping, lengthwise down the center of the baguette. Working quickly, open the oven door and generously spray the entire oven cavity with water (taking care not to spray the oven lightbulb) to create steam. (See "Creating Steam in Your Oven," page 17.) Slide the baguette onto the baking stone. Close the oven door. Bake 3 minutes. Open the oven door and spray all around the baguette. Close the oven door. Bake 3 minutes. Repeat spraying the oven walls. Close the oven door. Bake about 25 minutes, until the baguette is dark golden brown. Transfer the baguette to a wire rack and cool completely. (Repeat with the remaining baguettes.)

Makes 3 baguettes

BRIOCHE DOUGH

Brioche dough is used for sweet and savory applications. Because of the large quantity of butter and eggs in the dough, a longer kneading time is required to develop the gluten and to produce the fine-textured crumb that is the trademark of buttery brioche. We use this dough for sandwich buns, fruit tarts, and breakfast pastries.

Sponge

2¼ teaspoons active dry yeast

¼ cup lukewarm water (80°F)

½ cup milk

¾ cup all-purpose flour

Dough

3 cups all-purpose flour

½ cup granulated sugar

4 large eggs

2 large egg yolks

1 teaspoon fine sea salt

6 ounces (1½ sticks) unsalted butter, softened and cut up

Sponge

1. In a medium bowl, dissolve the yeast in the water and milk. Stir in the flour until combined. Cover the bowl and leave the sponge in a warm place (such as the top of the stove) until bubbly and active, about 2 hours.

Dough

2. Place the flour, sugar, eggs, egg yolks, and salt in the bowl of a heavy-duty mixer with a paddle attachment. Scrape the sponge over the top. Beat at low speed until thoroughly combined, 6 minutes. Add the butter. Increase the speed to medium; beat 15 minutes, until the butter is thoroughly incorporated and the dough is smooth, shiny, and elastic. Cover the dough and refrigerate overnight.

Makes 2½ pounds of dough

BRIOCHE SANDWICH BUNS

1 recipe Brioche Dough

1 large egg

1 teaspoon milk

10 teaspoons sesame seeds

1. Line 2 large baking sheets with parchment paper.

2. On a lightly floured surface, roll the brioche dough into a 20" log. Cut the log crosswise into 10 (2") pieces. Round each piece into a ball. Arrange 5 buns, 2" apart, on each prepared baking sheet. Flatten each lightly with the palm of your hand.

3. In a small bowl, whisk together the egg and milk. Brush the buns with the egg wash then sprinkle each with 1 teaspoon sesame seeds. Loosely drape a piece of plastic wrap over the buns; let rise in a warm, draft-free place (such as the top of the stove), until doubled in size, about 2 hours.

4. Meanwhile, position the oven racks in the upper and lower thirds of the oven. Preheat the oven to 400°F. Very quickly, open the oven door and generously spray the entire oven cavity with water (taking care not to spray the oven light-bulb) to create steam. Place both trays of buns in the oven. Close the oven door. Bake 1 minute. Open the oven door and spray all around the buns. Close the oven door. Bake 10 minutes. Open the oven and rotate the baking sheets between the oven racks. Bake until the buns are deep golden brown, 15 to 20 minutes more. Transfer the buns to a wire rack and cool completely.

Makes 10 buns

STICKY BUNS

We make this favorite American breakfast treat with brioche dough, which gives the buns a rich, yet light, texture. We prepare a separate amber-colored caramel to coat the buns, which ensures a smooth, chewy topping.

Topping

1 ¼ cups Caramel

¾ cup pecan halves

1 tablespoon currants

Buns

1 ½ pounds Brioche Dough (page 34)

8 tablespoons unsalted butter, melted and cooled

¾ cup firmly packed dark brown sugar

3 tablespoons Mexican ground cinnamon (see Resources, page 238)

1 ½ cups pecans, toasted and coarsely chopped (see "Toasting Nuts," page 137)

½ cup currants

1 large egg, lightly beaten

Topping

1. Coat an 8" × 3" round baking pan with vegetable cooking spray. Pour the caramel evenly over the bottom of the prepared pan. Sprinkle the pecans and currants evenly over the caramel. Set aside.

Buns

2. On a lightly floured surface, roll the brioche dough into a 12" × 20" rectangle. Arrange dough so that 1 long side is facing you. Brush the dough with 6 tablespoons of the melted butter. Spread the brown sugar evenly over the dough, then sprinkle the cinnamon, pecans, and currants evenly over the top. Drizzle the top with the remaining 2 tablespoons melted butter.

3. Brush the top edge of the dough opposite you with the beaten egg. Starting with the left corner of the edge closest to you, roll up the dough firmly (but not tightly) to form a log (similar to a jelly roll). Slice the log crosswise into 8 (2½") pieces (buns). Arrange

the buns, cut side up with the seam edges facing toward the center, in the prepared baking pan. (The buns should touch slightly.) Loosely drape a piece of plastic wrap over the buns. Let rise at room temperature until doubled in size, about 2 hours. (Or refrigerate the buns to rise slowly overnight.)

4. Meanwhile, preheat the oven to 325°F. Uncover the buns, place on the center oven rack. Bake 1 hour. Cool the buns in the baking pan on a wire rack 15 minutes. Place a serving platter or baking tray over the top of the baking pan and invert; remove the baking pan. Pull the buns apart to serve.

Makes 8 buns

CARAMEL

- 1 vanilla bean, split lengthwise
- 2 cups granulated sugar
- ½ cup water
- ½ tablespoon light corn syrup
- 1¼ cups heavy cream
- 2 tablespoons unsalted butter
- ⅛ teaspoon kosher salt

Scrape out the seeds of the vanilla bean. In a saucepan, stir together the vanilla bean and seeds, the sugar, water, and corn syrup. Cook over medium heat, stirring occasionally, until the sugar caramelizes to a light golden brown. With a long-handled spoon, quickly add the cream, butter, and salt. (The mixture will bubble vigorously, and the caramel will stiffen.) Reduce the heat; stir gently to re-melt the caramel. Cook 3 to 5 minutes or until slightly thickened. Cool. Transfer to an airtight container. (You may remove the vanilla bean at this point or leave it in.) The caramel can be refrigerated up to 2 weeks.

Makes 2½ cups

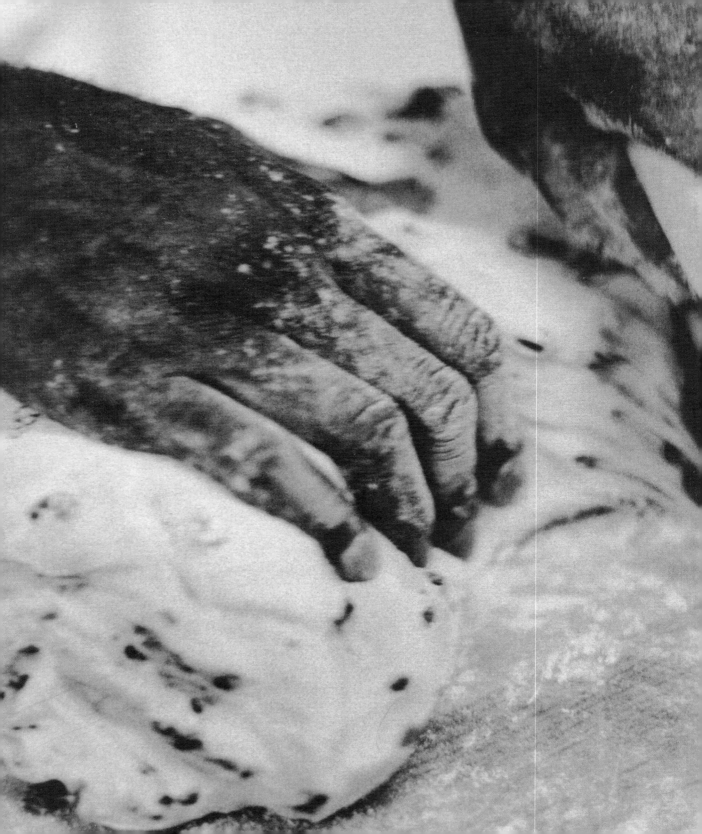

MUFFINS, SCONES, AND CEREAL

Muffins and scones are quick breads that can be cakelike and buttery rich or more wholesome with nuts and grains. They can be savory or sweet, and though usually eaten for breakfast or with tea, they might also be served with lunch or dinner. Most are easy to prepare and offer a great way to transform languid ingredients into delicious treats. While surveys indicate that the leading muffin flavors are blueberry, bran, and corn, we use what is available seasonally. In May and June, we may have strawberry muffins. In July and August, we serve blueberry scones. Deep into winter, apples and pears find their place in our muffins.

RAISIN-BRAN MUFFINS

Rich with molasses and honey, these muffins are great because they are light and moist despite their healthy quantity of bran and wheat germ.

2½ cups milk

½ cup firmly packed dark brown sugar

½ cup prune puree

¼ cup plus 1 tablespoon honey

¼ cup plus 1 tablespoon dark molasses

5 large eggs

¼ cup (½ stick) plus 2 tablespoons unsalted butter, melted and cooled

3¾ cups wheat bran

1 cup plus 2 tablespoons all-purpose flour

1 cup plus 2 tablespoons whole wheat flour

¾ cup wheat germ

3¾ teaspoons baking soda

1½ teaspoons kosher salt

3 cups dark raisins

1. Preheat the oven to 375°F. Butter twenty-four 2½" (½-cup) muffin-pan cups.

2. In large bowl, whisk together the milk, brown sugar, prune puree, honey, and molasses. Add the eggs and whisk until smooth. Stir in the melted butter until blended.

3. In another bowl, stir together the bran, all-purpose and whole wheat flours, wheat germ, baking soda, and salt. Stir the flour mixture into the brown sugar mixture just until blended. Stir in the raisins.

4. Spoon the batter evenly into the prepared muffin-pan cups. Bake 15 to 20 minutes, rotating the muffin pans between the upper and lower oven racks halfway through baking, until a wooden skewer inserted in the center of a muffin comes out clean. Cool the muffins in the pans for 5 minutes. Remove the muffins from the pans and cool completely on wire racks.

Makes 2 dozen muffins

CAPPUCCINO MUFFINS

We love the combination of espresso and bittersweet chocolate in this recipe. For a deeper, more intense chocolate flavor, we cut our own chocolate chips from a bar of good quality bittersweet chocolate.

¼ cup instant espresso powder

2¼ cups milk, heated until hot

2½ cups all-purpose flour

1¼ cups granulated sugar

1 tablespoon plus ½ teaspoon baking powder

1½ teaspoons ground cinnamon

½ teaspoon salt

2 large eggs

1 teaspoon vanilla extract

3 tablespoons unsalted butter, melted and cooled

1½ cups bittersweet chocolate chunks

1. Preheat the oven to 375°F. Butter twenty-four 2½" (½-cup) muffin-pan cups. Dissolve the espresso powder in the hot milk. Transfer to a medium bowl; set aside to cool.

2. In a large bowl, sift together the flour, sugar, baking powder, cinnamon, and salt. Whisk the eggs and vanilla into the cooled milk mixture, then whisk the milk mixture into the flour mixture just until blended. Stir in the melted butter. With a rubber spatula, fold in the chocolate chunks.

3. Spoon the batter evenly into the prepared muffin-pan cups. Bake 15 to 20 minutes, rotating the muffin pans between the upper and lower oven racks halfway through baking, until a wooden skewer inserted in the center of a muffin comes out clean. Cool the muffins in the pans for 5 minutes. Remove the muffins from the pans and cool completely on wire racks.

Makes 2 dozen muffins

LOW-FAT BERRY MUFFINS

Summer berries and yogurt are a great marriage. Here, they are combined to make a light, fragrant, low-fat muffin that our customers love.

1¼ cups fat-free milk

1¼ cups low-fat plain yogurt

½ cup canola oil

3 large eggs

Grated zest of 3 lemons

2 teaspoons vanilla extract

5 cups all-purpose flour

1¼ cups plus 2 tablespoons granulated sugar

2 tablespoons plus 2 teaspoons baking powder

2 teaspoons kosher salt

¼ teaspoon baking soda

2½ cups assorted fresh berries (such as raspberries, strawberries, or blueberries)

1. Preheat the oven to 375°F. Butter twenty-four 2½" (½-cup) muffin-pan cups.

2. In a large bowl, whisk together the milk, yogurt, oil, eggs, lemon zest, and vanilla. In another large bowl, stir together the flour, 1¼ cups of the sugar, baking powder, salt, and baking soda. Whisk the flour mixture into the yogurt mixture just until blended. With a rubber spatula, fold in the berries.

3. Spoon the batter evenly into the prepared muffin-pan cups; sprinkle on the remaining 2 tablespoons granulated sugar for the topping. Bake 15 to 20 minutes, rotating the muffin pans between the upper and lower oven racks halfway through baking, until a wooden skewer inserted in the center of a muffin comes out clean. Cool the muffins in the pans 5 minutes. Remove the muffins from the pans and cool completely on wire racks.

Makes 2 dozen muffins

APPLE-FILLED CARDAMOM MUFFINS

This rich, aromatic muffin utilizes one of India's finest spices, cardamom. Its pungent quality enhances the tart sweetness of the apple filling. The full flavor of the cardamom develops a few hours after the muffins have cooled.

Apple Filling

- 6 Granny Smith apples
- ¾ cup granulated sugar
- 3 tablespoons water
- ½ cinnamon stick
- Juice of 1 lemon

Batter

- 3½ cups all-purpose flour
- 1¾ cups granulated sugar
- 1 tablespoon baking powder
- 1 tablespoon cardamom
- 2 teaspoons kosher salt
- ½ cup firmly packed dark brown sugar
- 1½ cups (3 sticks) unsalted butter, cut into small cubes
- 2 cups heavy cream
- 1 cup sour cream
- 4 large eggs

Apple Filling

1. Peel, core, and chop 4 apples; combine the chopped apples in a nonreactive saucepan with the sugar, water, and cinnamon stick. Bring to a boil. Reduce the heat to low and simmer until the apples are very soft, about 12 minutes. Meanwhile, peel, core, and finely dice the remaining 2 apples.

2. Remove the saucepan from the heat. Press mixture with the back of a spoon to mash the apples. Stir in the diced apples and the lemon juice. Cook filling over low heat another 5 minutes. Set aside and cool.

3. Preheat the oven to 375°F. Butter twenty-four 2½" (½-cup) muffin-pan cups.

Batter

4. In the bowl of a heavy-duty mixer, sift together the flour, 1½ cups of the granulated sugar, baking powder, cardamom, and salt. Stir in the brown sugar. Add the butter to

the flour mixture and toss. With a paddle attachment at low speed, mix the butter into the flour mixture until the mixture resembles a coarse meal.

5. In a small bowl, whisk together the cream, sour cream, and eggs. At low speed, gradually add the cream mixture to the flour mixture just until blended and smooth. (Do not overmix.)

6. Fill the prepared muffin pan cups one-quarter of the way with the batter. Place 1 heaping tablespoon of the apple filling in the center of each cup, then top with the remaining batter. Sprinkle on the remaining ¼ cup granulated sugar. Bake 18 to 20 minutes, rotating the muffin pans between the upper and lower oven racks halfway through baking, until a wooden skewer inserted in the center of a muffin comes out clean. Cool the muffins in the pans 5 minutes. Remove the muffins from the pans and cool completely on wire racks.

Makes 2 dozen muffins

MILLET MUFFINS

This recipe was inspired by our visit to Café Fanny in Berkeley, California. We love the crunchiness that the millet adds to this simple brown sugar muffin.

4 cups all-purpose flour

2½ teaspoons baking powder

1½ teaspoons kosher salt

1 teaspoon baking soda

2 cups millet, lightly toasted and cooled (see "Toasting Millet")

6 large eggs

½ cup milk

2 teaspoons vanilla extract

¾ cup (1½ sticks) unsalted butter, softened

2 cups firmly packed dark brown sugar

1. Preheat the oven to 375°F. Butter twenty-four 2½" (½-cup) muffin-pan cups.

2. In a large bowl, sift together the flour, baking powder, salt, and baking soda. Stir in the millet. In a small bowl, whisk together the eggs, milk, and vanilla.

3. In the bowl of a heavy-duty mixer with a paddle attachment, beat the butter and brown sugar until light and fluffy. At low speed, add the flour mixture alternately with the egg mixture, beginning and ending with the flour mixture, just until blended. (Do not overmix.)

4. Spoon the batter evenly into the prepared muffin-pan cups. Bake 15 to 20 minutes, rotating the muffin pans between the upper and lower oven racks halfway through baking, until a wooden skewer inserted in the center of a muffin comes out clean. Cool the muffins in the pans 5 minutes. Remove the muffins from the pans and cool completely on wire racks.

Makes 2 dozen muffins

TOASTING MILLET

Millet, a grain that has been around for generations, is prized for its high protein content. Toasting it lightly will give this otherwise bland grain a crunchy texture and a nutty flavor. To toast, preheat the oven to 350°F. Spread the millet in an even layer on a baking sheet. Bake on the center oven rack 12 to 15 minutes, or until golden brown.

PUMPKIN-WALNUT MUFFINS

On the East Coast, pumpkin is a symbol of autumn's arrival. It is a favorite seasonal ingredient for pies, tarts, and cakes. Although some people prefer to make their own puree from sugar pumpkins, canned pumpkin is a fine substitute for this recipe.

4 cups all-purpose flour

1 tablespoon ground cinnamon

2 1/4 teaspoons baking powder

2 1/4 teaspoons baking soda

1 teaspoon salt

1/2 teaspoon ground ginger

1/2 teaspoon ground nutmeg

1/8 teaspoon ground cloves

2 cups granulated sugar

2 cups firmly packed dark brown sugar

10 tablespoons (1 1/4 sticks) cold unsalted butter, cut into small cubes

6 large eggs

2 1/4 cups pumpkin puree, fresh or canned (see "Preparing Pumpkin Puree")

3/4 cup milk

2 teaspoons vanilla extract

2 2/3 cups chopped walnuts, toasted (see "Toasting Nuts," page 137)

PREPARING PUMPKIN PUREE

To prepare pumpkin puree, preheat the oven to 375°F. Cut 1 sugar pumpkin in half and scoop out the seeds. Place the pumpkin halves cut-side down in a roasting pan. Add 1 cup water to the pan and bake 45 minutes or until the skin wrinkles. Remove the pumpkin from the pan. When cool enough to handle, scoop out the flesh. Press the flesh through a fine sieve set over a bowl. Clean the sieve, then line it with a double layer of cheesecloth and set it over another bowl. Spoon the puree into the sieve and drain in the refrigerator overnight.

1. Preheat the oven to 375°F. Butter twenty-four 2½" (½-cup) muffin-pan cups.

2. In the bowl of a heavy-duty mixer, sift together the flour, cinnamon, baking powder, baking soda, salt, ginger, nutmeg, and cloves. Stir in the granulated and brown sugars. Add the butter with the flour mixture and toss. With a paddle attachment at low speed, mix the butter into the flour mixture until the mixture resembles a coarse meal.

3. In a medium bowl, whisk the eggs; stir into the flour mixture. Stir in the pumpkin puree, milk, and vanilla, just until blended. With a rubber spatula, fold in the walnuts.

4. Spoon the batter evenly into the prepared muffin-pan cups. Bake 15 to 20 minutes, rotating the muffin pans between the upper and lower oven racks halfway through baking, until a wooden skewer inserted in the center of a muffin comes out clean. Cool the muffins in the pans 5 minutes. Remove the muffins from the pans and cool completely on wire racks.

Makes 2 dozen muffins

WHOLE WHEAT CHERRY SCONES

Stone-ground whole wheat flour and rolled oats give these scones a deeper flavor. The tart, dried cherries add a moist, chewy contrast.

3 cups all-purpose flour	3¾ cups old-fashioned oats
1½ cups whole wheat flour	Grated zest of 2 oranges
1¼ cups plus 2 tablespoons granulated sugar	2 cups (4 sticks) cold unsalted butter, cut into small cubes
1 tablespoon plus 1¼ teaspoons baking powder	1½ cups dried tart cherries (see Resources, page 238)
1½ teaspoons baking soda	1¼ cups buttermilk
1½ teaspoons kosher salt	2 tablespoons heavy or whipping cream

1. In the bowl of a heavy-duty mixer, combine the all-purpose and whole wheat flours, 1¼ cups of the granulated sugar, baking powder, baking soda, salt, oats, and orange zest. Add the butter to the flour mixture and toss. With a paddle attachment at low speed, mix the butter into the flour mixture until the mixture resembles a coarse meal. Stir in the dried cherries. Add the buttermilk and mix until the dough is evenly moistened and begins to come together.

2. Scoop the dough onto a lightly floured surface. With lightly floured hands, press the dough together into a ball. Divide the dough into 3 equal pieces. Gently round and flatten each piece into a ¾"-thick disk. Wrap each disk in plastic wrap and refrigerate for 2 hours or overnight.

3. When ready to bake, preheat the oven to 375°F. Line 2 large baking sheets with parchment paper or use nonstick baking sheets.

4. Unwrap the disks and place on a cutting board. Cut each disk into 6 equal wedges. Brush the tops lightly with the cream and sprinkle with the remaining 2 tablespoons granulated sugar. Separate the wedges, then transfer, 2" apart, to the prepared baking sheets. Bake 25 minutes, rotating the baking sheets between the upper and lower oven racks halfway through baking, or until golden. Cool on wire racks. Serve slightly warm.

Makes 1½ dozen scones

FIG-OAT SCONES

We prefer using dried Black Mission figs for this recipe because they have a firm texture and a subtle sweetness.

4⅔ cups all-purpose flour

1 cup plus 2 tablespoons granulated sugar

1½ teaspoons baking powder

1½ teaspoons kosher salt

Grated zest of 2 lemons

3 cups old-fashioned oats

2 cups (4 sticks) cold unsalted butter, cut into small cubes

1½ cups dried Black Mission figs, stems removed and cut into thirds

1½ cups buttermilk

2 tablespoons heavy or whipping cream

1. In the bowl of a heavy-duty mixer, combine the flour, 1 cup of the granulated sugar, baking powder, salt, lemon zest, and oats. Add the butter to the flour mixture and toss. With a paddle attachment at low speed, mix the butter into the flour mixture until the mixture resembles a coarse meal. Stir in the figs. Add the buttermilk and mix until the dough is evenly moistened and begins to come together.

2. Scoop the dough onto a lightly floured surface. With lightly floured hands, press the dough together into a ball. Divide the dough into 3 equal pieces. Gently round and flatten each piece into a ¾"-thick disk. Wrap each disk in plastic wrap and refrigerate for 2 hours or overnight.

3. When ready to bake, preheat the oven to 375°F. Line 2 large baking sheets with parchment paper or use nonstick baking sheets.

4. Unwrap the disks and place on a cutting board. Cut each disk into 6 equal wedges. Brush the tops lightly with the cream and sprinkle with the remaining 2 tablespoons granulated sugar. Separate the wedges, then transfer, 2" apart, to the prepared baking sheets. Bake 1 sheet of the scones at a time on the center oven rack, 25 minutes, or until golden. Cool on wire racks. Serve slightly warm.

Makes 1½ dozen scones

ORANGE-CURRANT SCONES

James perfected this recipe while he was the pastry chef at the White Dog Café. The currants, buttermilk, and orange zest add a subtle dimension to this traditional teatime food. Scones taste best when the dough is made the day before and refrigerated for 12 to 24 hours before being baked.

4 cups all-purpose flour

½ cup granulated sugar

2 teaspoons baking powder

2 teaspoons baking soda

¼ teaspoon kosher salt

Grated zest of 2 oranges

1 cup (2 sticks) cold unsalted butter, cut into small cubes

1½ cups dried black currants

¾ cup buttermilk

2 large eggs

2 tablespoons heavy or whipping cream

1. In the bowl of a heavy-duty mixer, combine the flour, sugar, baking powder, baking soda, salt, and orange zest. Add the butter to the flour mixture and toss. With a paddle attachment at low speed, mix the butter into the flour mixture until the mixture resembles a coarse meal. Stir in the currants.

2. In a small bowl, whisk together the buttermilk and eggs; pour over the flour mixture and beat at low speed until the dough is evenly moistened and comes together. Scoop the dough onto a piece of plastic wrap; flatten into a 21" × 4" rectangle. Wrap the dough and refrigerate 2 hours or overnight.

3. Meanwhile, preheat the oven to 375°F. Line 2 large baking sheets with parchment paper or use nonstick baking sheets.

4. Unwrap the chilled dough; place on a cutting board. Cut the dough crosswise into 7 (3") strips, then cut each strip into 2 triangles. Brush the tops with cream. Separate the triangles, then transfer, 2" apart, to the prepared baking sheets. Bake 20 to 25 minutes, rotating the baking sheets between the upper and lower oven racks halfway through baking, until golden. Cool on wire racks. Serve slightly warm.

Makes 14 scones

CRANBERRY-ALMOND OAT CEREAL

We developed this cereal recipe for our customers who wanted a nutritious breakfast alternative. The crunchy clusters of oats, almonds, and wheat germ provide a healthy, flavorful foundation for any morning.

¾ cup canola oil

½ cup honey

½ cup pure maple syrup

1 teaspoon vanilla extract

½ teaspoon almond extract

3½ cups old-fashioned oats

1½ cups sliced almonds

1 cup wheat germ

½ cup dry milk powder

1 teaspoon ground cinnamon

⅛ teaspoon ground cloves

1 cup dried cranberries (see Resources, page 238)

1. Preheat the oven to 275°F. In a medium saucepan, stir together the oil, honey, and maple syrup. Place over low heat and bring just to a simmer. (Do not boil.) Remove the pan from the heat and stir in the vanilla and almond extracts. Set aside.

2. In a large bowl, combine the oats, almonds, wheat germ, milk powder, cinnamon, and cloves. Pour the warm honey mixture over the top, then toss to coat the nuts and grains. Divide the nut and grain mixture onto 2 nonstick baking trays. Spread each into a thin layer.

3. Bake the cereal 20 minutes; remove the pans from the oven and stir. Spread the cereal again and bake 15 minutes more or until light golden. Cool the cereal completely on the pans so it becomes crisp. Stir in the cranberries. Store in an airtight container.

Makes 12 cups

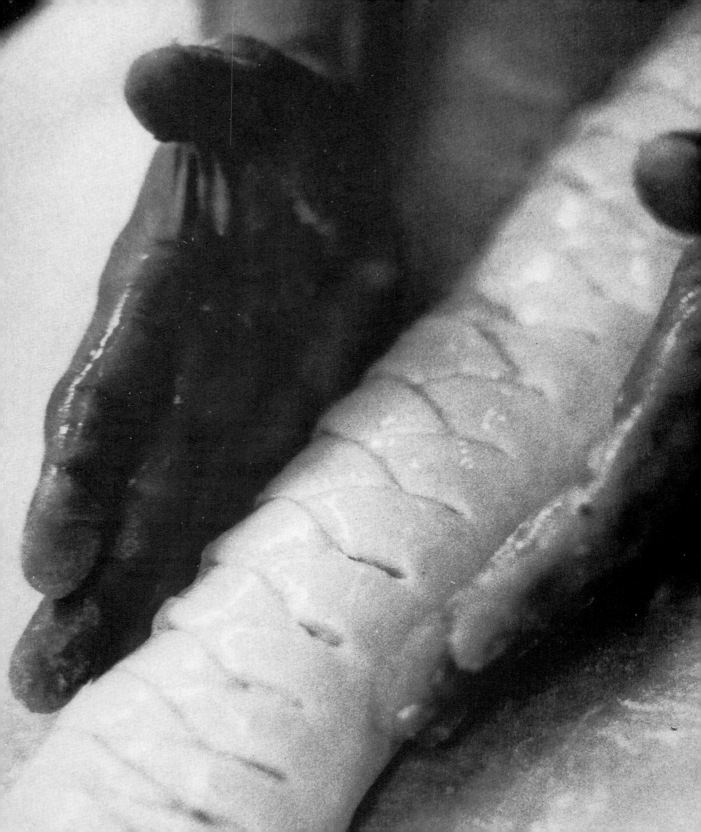

CROISSANTS AND DANISH

While the recipes in this chapter are labor intensive and time consuming, they will provide the home baker with a foundation for making multilayered dough. Some of the recipes may seem daunting, but once the basic techniques are mastered, everything from puff pastry to perfect buttery croissants is within reach. Each of the recipes in this chapter utilizes the same technique of rolling cold butter into a dough, working with a series of folds to produce a crisp, flaky, tender dough. While the method is similar for each of the recipes, the final pastries are distinct.

PUFF PASTRY DOUGH

The secret to the best puff pastry is using the best quality butter. Choose a butter that is high in fat and low in moisture content, qualities that are essential to producing a truly flaky croissant, Danish or puff pastry. The buttery and flaky layers of puff pastry are created not with yeast but by the folds of butter that are encased in the pastry dough following a process of "turning." Layers of butter become trapped within the dough. When these layers are introduced to the heat of the oven, the butter melts, creating steam and causing the dough to puff into hundreds of flaky layers.

3¾ cups all-purpose flour, plus flour for preparation

¼ cup granulated sugar

1 teaspoon kosher salt

3 cups (6 sticks) plus 3 tablespoons cold unsalted butter

1 teaspoon fresh lemon juice

1½ cups cold water

¼ cup heavy or whipping cream

1. *Détrempe* (base dough): In the bowl of a heavy-duty mixer, combine the flour, sugar, and salt. Cut the 3 tablespoons of cold butter into small cubes. With a dough hook attachment at low speed, mix the cubed butter into the flour mixture until it is the size of small peas and equally distributed. Toss in the lemon juice. In a small bowl, stir together the water and heavy cream. Mix the cream mixture into the flour mixture until the dough becomes smooth, about 1 minute. Shape the détrempe into a small rectangle; wrap in plastic wrap and refrigerate 2 hours or overnight.

2. *Bourrage* (butter block): Place the remaining 3 cups cold butter on a lightly floured surface. Working quickly to keep the butter cold, with a rolling pin, gently pound the butter into an 8" square (see photo 1, page 60). Place the bourrage on a tray in the refrigerator until firm but not too hard, about 10 minutes. (The bourrage and the détrempe should be equally pliant.)

3. Unwrap the détrempe. On a lightly floured surface, roll the détrempe into a 10" × 12" rectangle, leaving a slight mound in the center. Remove the bourrage from

the tray and place in the center of the dough (see photo 2, page 60). Lift and gently stretch each side of the dough over the bourrage, until the edges of the dough meet in the center. Press the edges to seal, enclosing the bourrage (see photo 3, page 60).

4. Roll the dough package lightly to anchor the dough with the butter (see photo 4, page 60). Sprinkle the dough package lightly with flour and gently roll into a 10" × 21" rectangle (see photo 5, page 60). With 1 long side facing you, fold the left edge of the dough over to the center of the rectangle, then fold the right edge over to the opposite side (see photos 6 and 7, page 61). Turn the dough 90°, so that 1 long side faces you again. Sprinkle the dough lightly with flour and gently roll again into a 10" × 21" rectangle. Fold the left edge over to the center of the rectangle, then fold the right edge over to the opposite side. Mark the folded dough with 2 finger imprints indicating that 2 "turns" have been completed. (Refrigerate the dough if it becomes too soft at any point while rolling or turning.) Wrap the dough in plastic wrap and refrigerate for at least 2 hours or overnight.

5. Repeat turning the dough 4 more times, refrigerating the dough for at least 1 hour after every 2 turns, until 6 turns are completed. After each turn, mark the dough with an imprint to remind yourself of the number of turns that have been made (see photo 9, page 61). If you choose to complete this entire process in 1 day, be aware that each time you roll the dough, the gluten will develop, making the dough more difficult to roll. We find it better to plan ahead and complete the turns over 2 or 3 days, giving the dough time to relax. Once the dough is completed, wrap it in plastic wrap then foil and freeze for up to 2 weeks.

Makes 4 pounds of dough

PREPARING PASTRY AND CROISSANT DOUGHS

1) On a lightly floured surface, soften the bourrage with a rolling pin.

2) Place the bourrage in the center of the détrempe.

3) Fold the détrempe over to encase the bourrage.

4) Anchor the bourrage with a rolling pin.

5) Roll the dough into a rectangle.

6) Fold the left edge over to the center of the rectangle.

7) Fold the right edge over to the opposite side.

8) The first turn completed.

9) Four finger imprints indicate the completion of four turns. Two turns remain for the completion of puff pastry dough.

Note:

Puff pastry dough uses 6 turns for a total of 6 imprints; croissant dough uses 4 turns for a total of 4 imprints.

CROISSANT DOUGH

Croissants were originally made from rich bread dough. Now they are made with yeasted pastry dough. The flaky layers are created both by the butter, which is trapped between the layers of the dough, creating steam, and by the yeast. Metropolitan's croissant dough includes our White Starter (page 9), which does not impart a sour taste but rather enhances the butter flavor.

---

3 cups bread flour, plus extra for preparation

1 cup all-purpose flour

2 tablespoons granulated sugar

1 teaspoon kosher salt

1¾ cups plus 2 tablespoons cold unsalted butter

⅔ cup lukewarm water (80°F)

2 teaspoons active dry yeast

⅔ cup cold milk

⅔ cup White Starter (page 9)

1. *Détrempe* (base dough): In the bowl of a heavy-duty mixer, combine the bread flour, all-purpose flour, sugar, and salt. Cut the 2 tablespoons of butter into small cubes. With a dough hook attachment at low speed, mix the cubed butter into the flour mixture until it is the size of small peas and equally distributed. In a medium bowl, stir together the water and yeast until the yeast dissolves. Stir in the milk and starter. Mix the milk mixture into the flour mixture, until the dough becomes smooth, about 1 minute. Shape the détrempe into a small rectangle; wrap in plastic wrap and refrigerate 2 hours or overnight.

2. *Bourrage* (butter block): Place the remaining 1¾ cups cold butter on a lightly floured surface. Working quickly to keep the butter cold, with a rolling pin, gently pound the butter into an 8" square (see photo 1, page 60). Place the bourrage on a tray in the refrigerator until firm but not too hard, about 10 minutes. (The bourrage and the détrempe should be equally pliant.)

3. Unwrap the détrempe. On a lightly floured surface, roll the détrempe into a 12" × 15" rectangle, leaving a slight mound in the center. Remove the bourrage from

the tray and place in the center of the dough (see photo 2, page 60). Lift and gently stretch each side of the dough over the bourrage, until the edges of the dough meet in the center. Press the edges to seal, enclosing the bourrage (see photo 3, page 60).

4. Roll the dough package lightly to anchor the dough with the butter (see photo 4, page 60). Sprinkle the dough package lightly with flour and gently roll into a 12" × 18" rectangle (see photo 5, page 60). With 1 long side facing you, fold the left edge of the dough over to the center of the rectangle, then fold the right edge over to the opposite side (see photos 6 and 7, page 61). Turn the dough 90°, so that 1 long side faces you again. Sprinkle the dough lightly with flour and gently roll again into a 12" × 18" rectangle. Fold the left edge over to the center of the rectangle, then fold the right edge over to the opposite side. (Refrigerate the dough if it becomes too soft at any point while rolling or turning.) Wrap the dough in plastic wrap and refrigerate for at least 2 hours or overnight. Mark the folded dough with 2 finger imprints indicating that 2 "turns" have been completed.

5. Repeat turning the dough 2 more times, so that 4 turns are completed. Refrigerate the dough at least 1 hour after every 2 turns. After each turn, mark the dough with an imprint to remind yourself of the number of turns that have been made (see photo 9, page 61). If you choose to complete this entire process in 1 day, be aware that each time you roll the dough, the gluten will develop, making the dough more difficult to roll. We find it better to plan ahead and complete the turns over 2 or 3 days, giving the dough time to relax. Once the dough is completed, wrap it in plastic wrap then foil and freeze for up to 2 weeks.

Makes 3 1/2 pounds of dough

PLAIN CROISSANTS

You'll get a much richer flavor and very crispy, flaky croissants if you allow them to rise slowly in the refrigerator overnight.

½ recipe Croissant Dough (page 62)

1 large egg

1 large egg yolk

1 tablespoon milk

¼ cup confectioners' sugar

1. Line 2 large baking sheets with parchment paper.

2. On a lightly floured surface, roll the croissant dough into a 12" × 24" rectangle. Cut the rectangle lengthwise in thirds, then crosswise in half to form six (4" × 12") rectangles. Cut each rectangle diagonally so you have 12 triangles (see photo 1). Arrange each triangle so the wide edge faces you. Roll each triangle up from the wide edge toward the tip (see photo 2). Lift and gently stretch the tip to ensure proper alignment of the rolls (see photo 3). Pinch the tip to seal (see photo 4). Bend the ends away from the tip to form a crescent shape. Arrange 6 croissants, seam-side down and 2" apart, on each prepared baking sheet.

3. Egg wash: In a small bowl, whisk together the egg, egg yolk, and milk. Lightly brush the tops and sides of the croissants with the egg wash. Loosely drape a piece of plastic wrap over the croissants; let rise in a warm, draft-free place (such as the top of the stove), until doubled in size, about 1 hour. (Or refrigerate the croissants to rise slowly overnight. The next day, let the croissants come to room temperature to finish rising, approximately 1 hour.) Refrigerate the egg wash.

4. Preheat the oven to 350°F. Uncover the croissants; gently brush the tops and sides again with the egg wash. Sift the confectioners' sugar over the croissants. Place 1 sheet of croissants on the center oven rack. Immediately reduce the oven temperature to 325°F. Bake 30 to 35 minutes, rotating the baking sheet front to back, until golden brown. Transfer the croissants to wire racks to cool. Repeat with the remaining croissants. Serve warm with butter and jam.

Makes 1 dozen croissants

1) Begin with 12 triangles of croissant dough.

2) Begin rolling the croissant with the wide edge of the triangle facing you.

3) Lift and gently stretch the tip to ensure proper alignment of the rolls.

4) Pinch the tip to seal the folded dough.

5) Rolled croissants ready to be transferred to trays for final rise.

ALMOND CROISSANTS

The combination of crunchy caramelized almonds and a moist almond center makes this croissant a pleasure to eat.

½ recipe Croissant Dough (page 62)

¾ cup Frangipane Cream (page 68)

1 large egg

1 large egg yolk

1 tablespoon milk

1 cup sliced blanched almonds

¼ cup confectioners' sugar

1. Line 2 large baking sheets with parchment paper.

2. On a lightly floured surface, roll the croissant dough into a 12" × 24" rectangle. Cut the rectangle lengthwise in thirds, then crosswise in half to form six (4" × 12") rectangles. Cut each rectangle diagonally so you have 12 triangles. Arrange each triangle so the long side faces you. Place 1 tablespoon of the frangipane in the center along the long side of each triangle, then fold the 2 bottom points over the frangipane so that they overlap. Roll each triangle up from the bottom toward the tip; pinch the tip to seal. Bend the ends away from the tip to form a crescent shape.

3. Egg wash: In a shallow bowl, whisk together the egg, egg yolk, and milk. Spread the almonds on a plate. Pick up each croissant with the seam side facing your palm. Dip each into the egg wash, then into the almonds. Roll each croissant back and forth in the almonds, pressing firmly enough so the nuts adhere. (Don't worry if the croissants flatten slightly.)

4. Arrange 6 croissants, seam-side down and 2" apart, on each prepared baking sheet. Lightly brush the tops and sides of the croissants with the egg wash; sift half the confectioners' sugar over the tops. Loosely drape a piece of plastic wrap over the croissants; let rise in a warm, draft-free place (such as the top of the stove), until doubled in size, about 1 hour. (Or refrigerate the croissants to rise slowly overnight. The next day, let the croissants come to room temperature to finish rising, approximately 1 hour.) Refrigerate the egg wash.

5. Preheat the oven to 350°F. Uncover the croissants; gently brush the tops and sides again with the egg wash. Sift the remaining confectioners' sugar over the tops. Place 1 sheet of croissants on the center oven rack. Immediately reduce the oven temperature to 325°F. Bake 30 to 35 minutes, rotating the baking sheet front to back, until golden brown and the almonds are caramelized. Transfer the croissants to wire racks to cool. Repeat with the remaining croissants.

Makes 1 dozen croissants

FRANGIPANE CREAM

4 cups whole blanched almonds

2 cups small pieces of stale bread
(French baguette)

1½ cups (3 sticks) unsalted butter

1 cup granulated sugar

3 ounces almond paste

2 large eggs

1 teaspoon almond extract

⅓ cup Pastry Cream

1. Preheat the oven to 325°F. Spread the almonds on a baking tray and bake until golden brown, about 12 minutes. Cool.

2. Spread the bread on another baking tray and bake 12 to 15 minutes, or until toasted. Cool.

3. Place toasted almonds and bread into the bowl of a food processor and process to a fine crumb.

4. In the bowl of a heavy-duty mixer with a paddle attachment, beat the butter and the sugar until creamy. Beat in the almond paste until well blended. Add eggs one at a time, beating well after each addition. With the mixer at low speed, stir in the almond extract, then add the ground almonds and bread crumbs. Add the pastry cream and blend well. Place the frangipane in an airtight container and store in the refrigerator up to 2 weeks.

Makes 6 cups

PASTRY CREAM

1 vanilla bean, split lengthwise

¾ cup milk

¾ cup heavy cream

4 large egg yolks

½ cup granulated sugar

3 tablespoons all-purpose flour

2 tablespoons cornstarch

⅛ teaspoon kosher salt

1 tablespoon unsalted butter

1. Scrape out the seeds of the vanilla bean. In a medium nonreactive saucepan, combine the vanilla bean and seeds, the milk, and cream. Bring the milk mixture to a simmer over medium heat. Remove the pan from the heat. Cover the pan and steep the milk mixture 15 minutes.

2. Meanwhile, in a large bowl whisk together the egg yolks, sugar, flour, cornstarch, and salt.

3. Return the milk mixture to a simmer over medium heat. Gradually whisk it into the egg mixture until blended. Pour the pastry cream back into the saucepan and whisk over medium heat until thickened. Strain the pastry cream through a fine sieve into a bowl. (Rinse and dry the vanilla bean. Reserve for another use.) Whisk in the butter. Place a piece of plastic wrap directly on the surface of the pastry cream (this will prevent a skin from forming). Refrigerate until thoroughly chilled. It can be refrigerated up to 1 week.

Makes 3 cups

PEAR AND BLUE CHEESE CROISSANT TART

We love this versatile tart because it can be eaten for breakfast, for lunch with a salad, or for dessert. Not overly sweet, the mellow flavor of the pears is the perfect contrast with the pungent blue cheese.

4 tablespoons unsalted butter

¼ recipe Croissant Dough (page 62)

1 large egg

1 large egg yolk

1 tablespoon milk

3–4 ripe pears (Bosc or Comice)

⅓ cup granulated sugar

2 ounces blue cheese, crumbled

2 tablespoons fresh lemon juice

2 tablespoons confectioners' sugar

1. Line a large baking sheet with parchment paper. Coat the bottom and sides of a 14" × 4½" tart pan with a removable bottom with 1 tablespoon of the butter.

2. On a lightly floured surface, roll the croissant dough into a 16" × 6½" rectangle. Line the prepared tart pan with the dough, pressing the dough in the corners and up against the sides of the pan. Trim off any overhang so the edge of the dough is flush with the rim of the pan. (Wrap and refrigerate the scraps for another use, such as cinnamon buns.)

3. Egg wash: In a small bowl, whisk together the egg, egg yolk, and milk. Brush the tart shell with the egg wash.

4. Cut the stems off the pears and slice each in half lengthwise. Scoop out seeds and trim the bottom end of each half. Slice each half lengthwise into ⅛"-thick slices. Arrange the pears in overlapping slices down the center of the tart shell. Sprinkle the slices with the granulated sugar. Dot the top with the remaining 3 tablespoons butter and the blue cheese. Drizzle the lemon juice over the fruit, then sift the confectioners' sugar over the top. Transfer the tart in the pan to the prepared baking sheet. Loosely drape a piece of plastic wrap over the top. Let rise in a warm, draft-free place (such as the top of the stove) until doubled in size, about 1 hour.

5. Meanwhile, preheat the oven to 350°F. Uncover the tart, place on the center oven rack. Immediately reduce the oven temperature to 325°F. Bake 30 to 40 minutes, rotating the baking sheet front to back, until golden brown. Cool the tart in the pan 10 minutes. Carefully remove the tart from the pan and cool completely on a wire rack.

Makes 1 tart

DANISH DOUGH

Danish dough is similar to croissant dough except it is further enriched by the addition of eggs, egg yolks, grated orange zest, and our favorite spice, cardamom. It can be rolled into a variety of twisted shapes and garnished with a plethora of fillings (recipes follow).

3¾ cups all-purpose flour, plus for preparation

½ cup granulated sugar

2 teaspoons ground cardamom

1 teaspoon kosher salt

⅛ teaspoon freshly grated nutmeg

1½ cups (3 sticks) plus 2 tablespoons cold unsalted butter

½ cup plus 3 tablespoons milk

2 teaspoons active dry yeast

¾ cup White Starter (page 9)

2 large egg yolks

1 large egg

1 tablespoon grated orange zest

1 teaspoon vanilla extract

1. *Détrempe* (base dough): In the bowl of a heavy-duty mixer, combine the flour, sugar, cardamom, salt, and nutmeg. Cut the 2 tablespoons of cold butter into small cubes. With a dough hook attachment at low speed, mix the cubed butter into the flour mixture until it is the size of small peas and equally distributed. In a medium bowl, stir together the milk and the yeast until the yeast dissolves. Stir in the starter, egg yolks, egg, orange zest, and vanilla. Mix the milk mixture into the flour mixture, until the dough forms a shaggy mass. Shape the détrempe into a small rectangle; wrap in plastic wrap and refrigerate 2 hours or overnight.

2. *Bourrage* (butter block): Place the remaining 1½ cups cold butter between 2 sheets of waxed paper. Working quickly to keep the butter cold, with a rolling pin, gently pound the butter into a 6" square. Place the bourrage on a tray in the refrigerator until firm but not too hard, about 10 minutes. (The bourrage and the détrempe should be equally pliant.)

3. Unwrap the détrempe. On a lightly floured surface, roll the détrempe into an 8" × 10" rectangle, leaving a slight mound in the center. Remove the bourrage from the tray and place in the center of the dough. Lift and gently stretch each side of the dough over the bourrage, until the edges of the dough meet in the center. Press the edges to seal, enclosing the bourrage.

4. Roll the dough package lightly to anchor the dough with the butter. Sprinkle the dough package lightly with flour and gently roll into a 12" × 18" rectangle. With 1 long side facing you, fold the left edge of the dough over to the center of the rectangle, then fold the right edge over to the opposite side. Turn the dough 90°, so that 1 long side faces you again. Sprinkle the dough lightly with flour and gently roll again into a 12" × 18" rectangle. Fold the left edge over to the center of the rectangle, then fold the right edge over to the opposite side. Mark the folded dough with 2 finger imprints indicating that 2 "turns" have been completed. (Refrigerate the dough if it becomes too soft at any point while rolling or turning.) Wrap the dough in plastic wrap and refrigerate for at least 2 hours or overnight. You now have completed 2 "turns."

5. Repeat turning the dough 2 more times, so that 4 turns are completed. Refrigerate the dough for at least 1 hour. After each turn, mark the dough with an imprint to remind yourself of the number of turns that have been made. If you choose to complete this entire process in 1 day, be aware that each time you roll the dough, the gluten will develop, making the dough more difficult to roll. We find it better to plan ahead and complete the turns over 2 or 3 days, giving the dough time to relax. Once the dough is completed, wrap it in plastic wrap then foil and freeze up to 2 weeks.

Makes 3½ pounds of dough

CINNAMON SWIRL DANISH

Kids love this simple, yet sophisticated, Danish. It has an unadulterated buttery quality and a pleasing cinnamon swirl throughout. A drizzle of Vanilla Cream adds the perfect sweet touch.

¾ recipe Danish Dough (page 72)

½ cup (1 stick) unsalted butter, melted and cooled

2 tablespoons granulated sugar

1 tablespoon Mexican ground cinnamon (see Resources, page 238)

1 large egg

1 large egg yolk

1 tablespoon milk

3 tablespoons confectioners' sugar

¾ cup Vanilla Cream

1. Line 2 large baking sheets with parchment paper.

2. On a lightly floured surface, roll the Danish dough to a 12" × 24" rectangle. Arrange dough so that 1 long side is facing you. Brush top and sides of dough with the melted butter (see photo 1, page 77). In a small bowl, stir together the granulated sugar and the cinnamon. Sprinkle the sugar mixture over the right-hand half of the dough. Fold the left-hand half of the dough over the sugared half to close the dough like a book. Gently press the dough together with a rolling pin to seal (see photo 2, page 77). Cut the dough crosswise into twelve 1"-thick strips (see photo 3, page 77). Working 1 strip at a time, take each strip and pinch the ends between your thumb and forefinger. Twist the ends in opposite directions to form a rope (see photo 4, page 77). Firmly holding 1 end of the rope, coil the other end around it to make a swirl (see photo 5, page 77). Pinch the ends together underneath to seal the swirl (see photo 6, page 77). Arrange 6 Danish, 2" apart, on each prepared baking sheet.

3. Egg wash: In a small bowl, whisk together the egg, egg yolk, and milk. Brush the Danish with the egg wash and then sift the confectioners' sugar over the top.

4. Loosely drape a piece of plastic wrap over the Danish. Let rise in a warm, draft-free place (such as the top of the stove) until doubled in size, about 1 hour.

5. Preheat the oven to 325°F. Uncover the Danish, place 1 sheet on the center oven rack. Bake 25 to 30 minutes, rotating the baking sheet front to back, until golden brown. Transfer the Danish to wire racks to cool. Repeat with the remaining Danish. Drizzle each Danish with 1 tablespoon of the Vanilla Cream.

Makes 1 dozen Danish

VANILLA CREAM

1 cup confectioners' sugar

2 tablespoons heavy or whipping cream

2 teaspoons vanilla extract

In a small bowl, whisk together the sugar, cream, and vanilla until smooth.

Makes about 1 1/4 cups

MIXED BERRY DANISH

Prepare Cinnamon Swirl Danish as directed; after sifting the confectioners' sugar over the Danish in step 3, gently press the center of each to make a well.

Place 1 tablespoon Cheese Filling for Danish (page 76) into each indentation, then top each with 1 tablespoon Red Berry Jam (page 76).

RED BERRY JAM

5 pints fresh strawberries, hulled and halved

1¾ cups granulated sugar

1½ cups dried strawberries (see Resources, page 238)

¾ cup dried cranberries (see Resources, page 238)

¾ cup dried tart cherries (see Resources, page 238)

Grated zest and juice of 2 lemons

In a large nonreactive saucepan, stir together 3 pints of the strawberries and the sugar. Cook over medium heat until the fruit becomes juicy and the mixture begins to boil. Reduce the heat to low; simmer the mixture 10 minutes. Add the dried strawberries, the cranberries, cherries, and lemon zest and juice. Simmer 20 minutes, stirring occasionally to avoid scorching. (At this point, the jam should be fairly thick.) Stir in the remaining 2 pints strawberries. Simmer the jam over very low heat, 12 to 15 minutes more. Cool the jam to room temperature; transfer to a covered container and refrigerate up to 2 weeks.

Makes 1 quart

CHEESE FILLING FOR DANISH

3 (8-ounce) packages of cream cheese (preferably Philadelphia Brand), at room temperature

½ cup granulated sugar

2 large egg yolks

1 large egg

2 tablespoons all-purpose flour

1¼ teaspoons vanilla extract

In the bowl of a heavy-duty mixer with a paddle attachment, beat the cream cheese and sugar until blended. Add the egg yolks and the egg, beating well after each addition. Beat in the flour and vanilla. Refrigerate in an airtight container up to 2 weeks.

Makes 4 cups

1) Brush the top and sides of the Danish dough with melted butter.

2) Press the folded dough together with a rolling pin to seal.

3) Cut the dough crosswise into 12 1"-thick strips.

4) Twist the ends of the strips in opposite directions to form a rope.

5) Firmly holding one end of the rope, coil the other end around it to make a swirl.

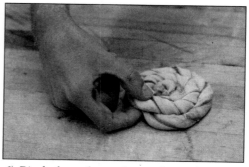

6) Pinch the ends together underneath to seal the swirl.

ESPRESSO–CHOCOLATE CHIP SWIRLS

These pastries are only sold at our bakery on weekends. They're just the ticket to satisfy cravings for coffee and chocolate.

½ recipe Puff Pastry Dough (page 58)

¾ cup unsalted butter, melted and cooled

1 cup granulated sugar

¾ cup instant espresso powder

2 cups bittersweet chocolate chunks

1 large egg

1 large egg yolk

1 tablespoon milk

2 tablespoons confectioners' sugar

½ cup crystal sugar

1. Line 2 large baking sheets with parchment paper.

2. On a lightly floured surface, roll the puff pastry dough to a 14" × 16" rectangle. Arrange the dough so that 1 long side is facing you. Brush the dough with half of the melted butter. Sprinkle the granulated sugar and espresso powder evenly over the dough, then sprinkle the chocolate chunks evenly over the top. Drizzle with the remaining melted butter.

3. Egg wash: In a small bowl, whisk together the egg, egg yolk, and milk. Brush the top edge of the dough opposite you with the egg wash. Starting with the edge closest to you, roll up the dough to form a log (similar to a jelly roll). Brush the entire log with the egg wash.

4. Slice the log crosswise into 12 equal rounds (swirls). Arrange 6 swirls, 2" apart, on each prepared baking sheet. Brush the swirls with the egg wash. Sift the confectioners' sugar over the tops, then sprinkle each with the crystal sugar. Refrigerate for 1 hour.

5. Preheat the oven to 375°F. Uncover the swirls, place 1 sheet on the center oven rack. Immediately reduce the oven temperature to 325°F. Bake 25 to 30 minutes, rotating the baking sheet front to back, until golden brown. Transfer the swirls to wire racks to cool. Repeat with the remaining swirls.

Makes 1 dozen swirls

MEYER LEMON AND BLUEBERRY TURNOVERS

The Meyer lemon and fresh blueberry filling in this flaky pastry is a surprising contrast to the more common fruit fillings.

Meyer Lemon Custard

¼ cup granulated sugar

1½ teaspoons all-purpose flour

¼ teaspoon kosher salt

¾ cup Meyer lemon juice (see note)

3 large eggs

3 large egg yolks

3 tablespoons butter, cut up

Grated zest of 3 Meyer lemons

Blueberry Jam

1 cup fresh blueberries

Juice of ½ Meyer lemon

1 tablespoon granulated sugar

½ cup plus 4½ teaspoons granulated sugar

½ recipe Puff Pastry Dough (page 58)

1 large egg, lightly beaten

Meyer Lemon Custard

1. In a medium nonreactive saucepan, stir together the granulated sugar, flour, and salt. Whisk in the lemon juice, eggs, and egg yolks until smooth. Cook over medium heat, stirring constantly, until the custard thickens. Strain the custard through a fine sieve into a bowl; whisk in the butter and lemon zest until blended. Cover the custard with plastic wrap and refrigerate until cold.

Blueberry Jam

2. In a small nonreactive saucepan, stir together half of the blueberries, the lemon juice, and 1 tablespoon of the granulated sugar. Cook over medium heat, stirring occasionally, until the blueberries start to pop and release their juices. Reduce the heat and simmer for 10 minutes. Remove the pan from the heat; stir in the remaining blueberries. Transfer the jam to a bowl; refrigerate until cooled.

3. Sprinkle ½ cup of the granulated sugar over a cool, flat surface; dust lightly with flour. Roll the puff pastry dough on the prepared surface into a 12" square. Cut the dough into nine 4" squares.

4. Line a large baking sheet with parchment paper. Brush the pastry squares lightly with the beaten egg. Place 1 tablespoon of the blueberry jam in the center of each square. Top each with 1 tablespoon lemon custard. Carefully fold 1 corner of the square over the filling to meet the opposite corner. Press the edges carefully to enclose the filling. Place the turnovers on the prepared baking sheet. Refrigerate uncovered 3 hours or overnight. Refrigerate the beaten egg.

5. Preheat the oven to 375°F. Brush the turnovers with the beaten egg, then sprinkle each with ½ teaspoon of the remaining sugar. Bake the turnovers on the center oven rack 30 to 35 minutes or until dark golden brown. Transfer to wire racks to cool slightly. Serve warm or at room temperature. (Do not refrigerate baked turnovers or they will lose their crispness.)

Makes 9 turnovers

Note:

Meyer lemons, native to Northern California, are now commercially produced in Florida and California. The best Meyer lemons are picked from established backyard trees. They are larger than the commercially grown lemons and have a much sweeter taste, a thicker rind, and a floral aroma. Meyer lemons are usually available in specialty food markets from mid-January until the end of March. If you use regular lemons in this recipe, use ½ cup regular lemon juice plus ¼ cup orange juice.

CAKES

*Our cakes are simple, homespun, and made according to our philos-
ophy of producing only what is in season and fresh. Variations might
include adding herbs, fruits, and nuts. They are not the fancy,
gelatin-style cakes found in many bakeries. Rather, they are simple
and rustic in nature. Though perfectly satisfying on their own, most
of the cakes at Metropolitan are designed to allow the customer to embellish them with ice creams, fruits, or sauces when they are served.*

CITRUS ANGEL FOOD CAKE

Angel food cake is a light, flavorful, low-fat dessert alternative. The abundance of citrus zest in this cake provides enough flavor to make one forget that this is eating light.

Cake

10	large egg whites, at room temperature
¼	teaspoon cream of tartar
1½	cups granulated sugar
1	cup all-purpose flour
⅛	teaspoon kosher salt
	Grated zest of 1 lemon

Grated zest of 1 orange

Grated zest of 1 lime

Citrus Glaze

1¼	cups confectioners' sugar
¼	cup fresh lemon juice
	Grated zest of 1 lime

Cake

1. Preheat the oven to 350°F.

2. In a large, clean, dry bowl of an electric mixer, combine the egg whites and cream of tartar. With a whip attachment at low speed, beat the whites until foamy. Increase the mixer speed to high; beat the whites until soft peaks form. Gradually add ¾ cup of the sugar, 1 tablespoon at a time, beating well after each addition. When all the sugar is incorporated, continue to beat until the mixture is shiny and just holds firm peaks when the beaters are lifted. (Do not overbeat.)

3. Sift together the remaining ¾ cup of sugar, the flour, and the salt onto a piece of parchment paper.

4. With a rubber spatula, gently fold the lemon, orange, and lime zests into the egg white mixture. Sift one-third of the flour mixture over the whites; gently fold in with the spatula. Repeat twice more with the remaining flour mixture just until blended. Pour the batter into an 8¼" × 4¼" angel food cake pan (see note). Gently run a knife through the batter to remove any air pockets.

5. Bake the cake on the center oven rack 40 to 45 minutes, until a skewer inserted in the center of the cake comes out clean. Immediately invert the pan onto a funnel or bottle. Let cool completely.

Citrus Glaze

6. Sift the confectioners' sugar into a small bowl. Add the lemon juice and lime zest; whisk until smooth.

7. Turn the cake pan right side up; run a spatula around the sides of the pan and tube. Invert the cake to unmold. Place the cake on a serving tray or cake stand. Pour the glaze over the top. Let the cake stand 15 minutes, until glaze sets.

Makes 1 (8¼") cake, 8 to 10 servings

Note:

An angel food pan is not buttered prior to being filled in order to allow the egg whites to expand and climb as the cake bakes.

FLOURLESS CHOCOLATE CAKE

Although this is our most popular cake all year, it is especially appreciated during Passover. Here it is simply dusted with confectioners' sugar but you may embellish the cake further with the Chocolate Glaze (page 111) that is used on the Chocolate "Mounds" Tart.

12 tablespoons (1½ sticks) unsalted butter, cut into small cubes

6 ounces bittersweet chocolate, chopped

½ cup unsweetened Dutch-process cocoa

¾ cup granulated sugar

4 large eggs, separated

¼ teaspoon kosher salt

1 tablespoon vanilla extract

Confectioners' sugar, for garnish

1. Preheat the oven to 350°F. Butter an 8" × 3" round cake pan; line the bottom with a parchment paper circle. Lightly butter the parchment paper.

2. Combine the butter and chocolate in a large heatproof bowl. Set the bowl over a saucepan halfway filled with barely simmering water.

3. Meanwhile, sift the cocoa and sugar into another bowl. In the large bowl of an electric mixer, combine the egg whites and salt. With a whip attachment at medium-high speed, beat the whites until soft peaks form. Set both aside.

4. Remove the melted butter and chocolate from the simmering water. Stir until smooth and to release the heat. Add the cocoa mixture, egg yolks, vanilla, and one-quarter of the beaten whites. Stir with a whisk until the mixture is smooth. With a rubber spatula, gently fold in the remaining whites just until blended. Pour the batter into the prepared pan. Bake the cake on the center oven rack 30 to 35 minutes, until a skewer inserted in the center of the cake just barely comes out clean.

5. Cool the cake on a wire rack. (The cake will rise in the oven. As the cake cools, it will collapse slightly. The surface of the cake will crack in a lovely irregular pattern.) To unmold, run a knife around the sides of the pan. Place a plate over the pan and invert. Remove the pan and the parchment paper. Invert the cake, right side up, onto a serving plate or cake stand. Garnish the cake with confectioners' sugar.

Makes 1 (8") cake, 6 to 8 servings

CHOCOLATE LAYER CAKE

Chocolate layer cake is the perfect comfort food. It subscribes to the principle that less is more! Mayonnaise is the salient ingredient in our extremely moist and sinfully rich chocolate cake.

½ cup unsweetened Dutch-process cocoa

1½ cups boiling water

1½ teaspoons vanilla extract

1½ cups Mayonnaise (page 90)

3 cups all-purpose flour

1½ cups granulated sugar

1 tablespoon baking soda

½ teaspoon kosher salt

1 recipe Chocolate Glaze (page 111)

1. Preheat the oven to 350°F. Butter a 9" × 3" cake pan; line the bottom with a parchment paper circle. Lightly butter the parchment paper.

2. In a bowl, whisk together the cocoa and boiling water. Whisk in the vanilla and mayonnaise. Set aside to cool.

3. In a large bowl, sift together the flour, sugar, baking soda, and salt. Whisk in the cocoa mixture until smooth. Pour the batter into the prepared pan. Bake the cake on the center oven rack 40 to 45 minutes, until a skewer inserted in the center of the cake comes out clean. Cool the cake in the pan on a wire rack. Wrap in plastic wrap and refrigerate overnight.

4. To unmold the cake, dip a knife in hot water, then carefully run it around the edge of the cake. Place a cutting board on top of the cake pan and invert. Remove the pan and the parchment paper; invert the cake right side up. With a warm serrated knife, trim the domed top of the cake so that the top is level. (Set aside the top for bread pudding.) With the knife, split the cake in 2 equal layers.

5. Stir the chocolate glaze until it is slightly thickened and just holds a shape when a spoon is lifted. Place the bottom layer, cut-side up, into the cake pan. Spread 1 cup of the

glaze evenly over the layer so that it reaches the sides of the pan. (Set the remaining glaze aside.) Place the remaining cake layer on top of the other layer in the pan. Gently press the top of the cake to make it level. Cover and refrigerate the cake 1 hour or overnight.

6. Place a wire rack on top of the cake pan and invert. Lift the pan from the cake. (The bottom of the cake now becomes the top.) Set the cake over a sheet of parchment paper.

7. Re-melt the remaining chocolate glaze over low heat. Cool slightly. Stir the glaze until slightly thickened; pour over the top of the cake. With an offset spatula, gently spread the glaze toward the edges of the cake, allowing it to run down the sides. Run the spatula around the sides of the cake to spread the glaze evenly. Carefully lift the cake onto a serving plate. Serve at room temperature.

Makes 1 (9") cake, 8 to 10 servings

MAYONNAISE

2 large egg yolks

½ teaspoon red-wine vinegar

⅛ teaspoon kosher salt

1½ cups canola oil

In a blender or food processor, process the egg yolks, vinegar, and salt until blended. With the machine running, slowly add the oil in a thin, steady stream through the feed tube, until it is incorporated and the mixture is emulsified.

Makes about 1 ¾ cups

Note:

This mayonnaise may be refrigerated up to 5 days. If the mayonnaise should break, transfer the broken mayonnaise to a glass measure. Place another egg yolk and 1 tablespoon warm water in the blender or food processor; process until blended. With the machine running, slowly add the broken mayonnaise through the feed tube until an emulsion is formed.

BANANA-NUT CAKE

If you have bananas on your counter that are getting black, don't despair. You can mash them up and make this moist, delicious cake.

1 pound ripe bananas, peeled and cut up

1¼ cups sour cream

2½ cups all-purpose flour

1 cup granulated sugar

2¼ teaspoons baking soda

1½ teaspoons baking powder

½ teaspoon kosher salt

1 cup (2 sticks) plus 2 tablespoons unsalted butter, softened

½ cup firmly packed dark brown sugar

1 tablespoon grated lemon zest

4 large eggs

1½ cups walnuts, toasted and coarsely chopped (see "Toasting Nuts," page 137)

1 cup coarsely chopped bittersweet chocolate

1 cup warm Chocolate Glaze (page 111)

1. Preheat the oven to 350°F. Butter a 10" Bundt pan or coat with nonstick spray.

2. In a food processor, process the bananas and sour cream until smooth. In a bowl, sift together the flour, sugar, baking soda, baking powder, and salt. Set both aside.

3. In a large bowl of an electric mixer with a paddle attachment, beat the butter and brown sugar until light and fluffy. Beat in the lemon zest. Add the eggs, one at a time, beating well after each addition. At low speed, beat one-third of the banana mixture into the butter mixture; repeat twice with the remaining banana mixture. Beat one-third of the flour mixture into the banana mixture; repeat twice with the remaining flour mixture. Beat the batter 30 seconds more or until smooth. Fold in the walnuts and chocolate. Pour the batter into the prepared pan.

4. Bake the cake on the center oven rack 50 to 55 minutes, until a skewer inserted into the center of the cake comes out clean. Cool the cake in the pan on a wire rack. Invert the cake onto a cake stand or serving plate; remove the pan. Pour the chocolate glaze over the top. Let the cake stand 10 minutes, until glaze sets.

Makes 1 (10") Bundt cake, 8 to 10 servings

CARROT CAKE

This moist, healthful cake is delicious for breakfast. You may omit the cream cheese glaze to prepare a lower-fat dessert.

Cake

1½ cups all-purpose flour

1½ teaspoons ground cinnamon

¼ teaspoon ground cloves

¼ teaspoon ground nutmeg

1½ teaspoons baking powder

1 teaspoon baking soda

1¼ cups extra-virgin olive oil

1½ cups granulated sugar

4 large eggs

3 cups grated carrots

¾ cup pecans, toasted and coarsely chopped (see "Toasting Nuts," page 137)

¾ cup golden raisins

½ cup walnuts, toasted and coarsely chopped (see "Toasting Nuts," page 137)

2 tablespoons hot water

Cream Cheese Glaze

4 tablespoons unsalted butter, softened

6 ounces cream cheese (preferably Philadelphia Brand), softened

¾ cup heavy cream

3 tablespoons confectioners' sugar

1 teaspoon fresh lemon juice

½ teaspoon vanilla extract

1. Preheat the oven to 350°F. Butter a 9" Bundt pan or coat with nonstick spray.

Cake

2. Sift together the flour, cinnamon, cloves, nutmeg, baking powder, and baking soda onto a piece of parchment paper. Set aside.

3. In a large bowl of an electric mixer with a whisk attachment, beat the oil and granulated sugar. Add the eggs, one at a time, beating well after each addition. At low speed, stir in the flour mixture just until combined. Add the carrots, pecans, raisins, walnuts, and water. Pour the batter into the prepared pan. Bake the cake on the center oven rack 40 to 45 minutes, until a skewer inserted into the center of the cake comes out clean. Cool the cake completely in the pan on a wire rack.

Cream Cheese Glaze

4. Meanwhile, in another bowl of an electric mixer, beat the butter until creamy. Add the cream cheese and beat until smooth. At low speed, beat in the cream, confectioners' sugar, lemon juice, and vanilla until the glaze is smooth and pourable.

5. Invert the cake onto a cake stand or serving plate; remove the pan. Drizzle the cake with the cream cheese glaze; let stand 10 minutes or until set.

Makes 1 (9") Bundt cake, 8 to 10 servings

BERRY CRUMB CAKE

This is the perfect brunch cake. Your friends will pick at the crumbs as they fall from the cake . . . as Wendy does when they arrive in the store!

Cake

- 1 cup plain yogurt
- 1 cup sour cream
- 2 large eggs
- 1 tablespoon vanilla extract
- 2¼ cups all-purpose flour
- 1 tablespoon plus ¾ teaspoon baking powder
- ½ teaspoon kosher salt
- 1 cup (2 sticks) unsalted butter, softened
- 1¾ cups granulated sugar
- Grated zest of 1 lemon

- 2 cups fresh berries (such as blueberries, raspberries, or blackberries)

Crumb Topping

- ¾ cup plus 2 tablespoons all-purpose flour
- ½ cup granulated sugar
- 1 teaspoon ground cinnamon
- ½ teaspoon kosher salt
- ¼ teaspoon baking powder
- 6 tablespoons unsalted butter, melted and cooled
- Confectioners' sugar, for garnish

1. Preheat the oven to 350°F. Butter a 9" × 3" round cake pan; line the bottom with a parchment paper circle. Lightly butter the parchment paper.

Cake

2. In a bowl, stir together the yogurt, sour cream, eggs, and vanilla. In another bowl, sift together the flour, baking powder, and salt.

3. In a large bowl of an electric mixer, beat the butter and sugar until light and creamy. Add the lemon zest; beat 1 minute. Add the yogurt mixture alternately with the flour mixture, beginning and ending with the flour mixture, and beating well after each addition. Spread the batter in the prepared pan. Sprinkle the berries over the top. Bake the cake on the center oven rack 40 minutes.

Crumb Topping

4. Meanwhile, in a bowl, stir together the flour, sugar, cinnamon, salt, and baking powder. Add the butter and toss until the mixture becomes crumbly.

5. Remove the cake from the oven; sprinkle the crumb topping over the cake. Bake the cake 15 to 20 minutes more, until a skewer inserted in the center comes out clean. Cool the cake on a wire rack. Run a knife around the edge of the cake. Place a plate over the pan and invert. Remove the pan and the parchment paper. Invert the cake, right side up, onto a serving plate or cake stand. Garnish the cake with confectioners' sugar.

Makes 1 (9") cake, 8 to 10 servings

MASCARPONE CHEESECAKE

Although neither of us were big fans of cheesecake, it is so popular that it was necessary for us to develop a recipe that would please both our customers and ourselves. Using Italian mascarpone and lightening the cake with whipped cream, we succeeded. You may also substitute whipped Crème Fraîche (page 133) for the whipped cream to add a pleasant tanginess to the recipe. The recipe adapts to individual-size cheesecakes as well.

1 recipe Sweet Pastry (page 104)	4 large eggs, at room temperature
2 pounds cream cheese (preferably Philadelphia Brand), softened	½ teaspoon vanilla extract
1¼ cups mascarpone cheese	¼ teaspoon kosher salt
1½ cups granulated sugar	½ cup heavy cream
1 tablespoon grated lemon zest	Fresh macerated berries

1. Preheat the oven to 350°F. Line the bottom of a 9" × 3" cake pan with a parchment paper circle.

2. On a lightly floured sheet of waxed paper, roll the pastry into a ¼"-thick circle. Using a cardboard cake circle as a guide, cut a 9" circle of pastry. Sprinkle the pastry lightly with flour and place the cardboard circle on top. Invert the paper so the pastry is right side up; remove the waxed paper. Gently slide the pastry into the prepared pan. (If the pastry tears, press together gently.) Chill. Follow instructions for baking pastry on page 107. Bake on the center oven rack 15 to 20 minutes, until the pastry is golden brown. Cool on a wire rack. Reduce the oven temperature to 325°F.

3. In a large bowl of an electric mixer with a paddle attachment, beat the cream cheese until light and fluffy. At low speed, add the mascarpone cheese and beat until blended. Gradually add the sugar, 1 tablespoon at a time, beating well after each addition. Beat in the lemon zest. Add the eggs, one at a time, beating well after each addition. Add vanilla and salt.

4. In a small bowl of an electric mixer, beat the cream to soft peaks. With a rubber spatula, fold the whipped cream into the cheese mixture. Pour the batter into the prepared cake pan on top of the baked pastry. Place the cake pan in a larger baking pan. Place the baking pan on the center oven rack. Carefully pour enough hot water into the baking pan so it comes two-thirds up the sides of the cake pan. Bake the cheesecake 50 minutes, or until cake barely jiggles in the center.

5. Remove the cake from the water bath. Cool completely on a wire rack. Cover and refrigerate the cake overnight. To unmold, dip a small knife in hot water. Run the knife around the edge of the cake. Place a plate over the pan and invert. Remove the pan and the parchment paper. Turn the cake right side up and place on a serving plate or cake stand. Serve with the berries.

Makes 1 (9") cake, 8 to 10 servings

UPSIDE DOWN PLUM ROSE GERANIUM CAKE

During our restaurant days, James developed this cake using organically grown herbs from our friends Mark and Judy Dornstreich at Branch Creek Farm. The rose geranium adds a floral and peppery component, which marries perfectly with plums. If rose geranium is not available, you can omit it from the recipe.

Fruit

2 tablespoons unsalted butter

½ cup firmly packed brown sugar

6 firm plums, halved and cut into eighths

Cake

1½ cups plus 2 tablespoons all-purpose flour

1 teaspoon baking powder

½ teaspoon kosher salt

⅓ cup plus 1 tablespoon sour cream

4 large eggs

1 tablespoon rose water

1 cup (2 sticks) unsalted butter

1½ cups granulated sugar

1 tablespoon grated lemon zest

⅓ cup organic rose geranium leaves, coarsely chopped

1. Preheat the oven to 350°F. In a heavy-bottomed 9" × 3" cake pan, combine the butter and brown sugar. Place over medium heat and stir until the mixture melts and begins to bubble. Remove the pan from the heat. Arrange the plum slices in tight concentric circles over the bottom of the pan. Return the pan to the heat; cook for 3 to 5 minutes or until the plums begin to release their juices. Remove the pan from the heat. Set aside.

Cake

2. In a bowl, sift together the flour, baking powder, and salt. In another bowl, whisk together the sour cream, eggs, and rose water. Set both aside.

3. In a large bowl of an electric mixer, beat the butter and granulated sugar until light and fluffy. Beat in the lemon zest. At low speed, add the sour cream mixture alternately with the flour mixture, beginning and ending with the flour mixture and beating well after each addition. Stir in the rose geranium leaves.

4. Pour the batter over the plums in the pan. Bake the cake on the center oven rack 35 minutes, until a skewer inserted in the center of the cake comes out clean. Cool the cake on a wire rack 10 minutes. Run a knife around the sides of the cake. Place a serving plate over the cake pan; carefully invert the cake and remove the pan. Serve warm or at room temperature.

Makes 1 (9") cake, 8 to 10 servings

GINGER SPICE CAKE

This complex and richly flavored cake is perfect to douse with whipped cream or sabayon. Although the directions given are for a typical round cake pan, you can make it in a square pan and cut it into squares, or even make small cakes in individual pans.

1¾	cups all-purpose flour	¾	cup granulated sugar
½	teaspoon ground cinnamon	¾	cup sunflower oil
¼	teaspoon ground cloves	2½	tablespoons grated fresh ginger
¼	teaspoon freshly ground black pepper	1½	teaspoons baking soda
⅛	teaspoon ground ginger	¾	cup boiling water
¾	cup dark molasses	2	large eggs

1. Preheat the oven to 350°F. Butter a 9" × 3" round cake pan; line the bottom with a parchment paper circle. Lightly butter the parchment paper.

2. In a large bowl, sift together the flour, cinnamon, cloves, pepper, and ground ginger. In another bowl, whisk together the molasses, sugar, oil, and ginger.

3. Whisk the molasses mixture into the flour mixture. In a bowl, stir the baking soda into the boiling water; whisk into the flour mixture. Add the eggs and whisk till smooth.

4. Place a fine sieve over a bowl; scrape the batter through the sieve. (This will ensure any strings from the freshly grated ginger are removed.) Pour the batter into the prepared pan. Bake the cake on the center oven rack 50 to 60 minutes, until a skewer inserted in the center of the cake comes out clean. Cool the cake completely in the pan on a wire rack. Run a knife around the edge of the cake. Place a plate over the pan and invert. Remove the pan and the parchment paper. Place a serving plate over the cake and invert the cake, right side up.

Makes 1 (9") cake, 6 to 8 servings

GALETTE BRETON

Throughout France, you frequently stumble upon these little butter cakes. They are made from a sweet pastry base or a yeasted bread base, depending on the region they come from. The real key is to use a buttery dough. Serve warm from the oven for an amazingly simple, yet delectable, treat!

4 tablespoons butter, melted

¾ pound Brioche Dough (page 34)

1 cup Crème Fraîche (page 133)

Grated zest of 1 lemon

6 tablespoons granulated sugar

6 teaspoons crystal sugar (see Resources, page 238)

1. Preheat the oven to 400°F. Line a large baking tray with parchment paper. Lightly brush the paper with the melted butter. Place six 4¼" × ¾" flan rings on the prepared tray. Butter the sides of the rings.

2. Divide the dough into 6 equal pieces. Lightly round each piece, then place each in a flan ring, gently pressing the dough to the sides of the rings. Cover loosely with plastic wrap and let rise at room temperature 1 hour.

3. In a bowl, combine the crème fraîche and lemon zest. When the dough has risen, press the dough slightly up the sides of the rings and dimple the centers with your fingertips. Place 2 heaping tablespoons crème fraîche in the center of each cake. Sprinkle each with 1 tablespoon granulated sugar, then 1 teaspoon crystal sugar.

4. Bake the cakes on the center oven rack 15 to 18 minutes, until golden brown. Cool 10 minutes. Carefully lift the flan rings from the cakes. Serve warm or at room temperature.

Makes 6 (4¼") cakes

PIES AND TARTS

Making a pie or tart is not difficult. It's all a matter of perfecting a simple pie dough recipe. The rest is easy. We combine butter and shortening to create a wonderfully flaky crust that can be filled with both sweet and savory ingredients. The key is always to use seasonal ingredients. You won't find a strawberry pie on our shelves in the middle of winter, for example. Just because berries and peaches are sold year-round in most grocery stores doesn't mean it's a good idea to eat them—or to use them in your pie or tart. April is the first sign that spring is near and is when berries and asparagus become available. That is also the time when Meyer lemons and citrus fruits are ending. In fall, apples and pumpkins inspire our recipes. Let a trip to your local farmers' market guide you to seasonal ingredients for these recipes.

SWEET PASTRY

¼ cup cold water

2 large egg yolks

1 teaspoon vanilla extract

1½ cups all-purpose flour

¼ cup granulated sugar

½ teaspoon kosher salt

1 cup (2 sticks) cold unsalted butter, cut into small cubes

1. In a small bowl, stir together the water, egg yolks, and vanilla. Set aside.

2. In a large bowl of an electric mixer, combine the flour, sugar, and salt. With a paddle attachment at low speed, mix the butter into the flour mixture until the mixture resembles a coarse meal. Add the egg mixture and mix just until the dough begins to hold together. (Do not overmix. The dough will begin to stick to the mixer paddle. It will look crumbly but feel moist.)

3. Turn the dough out onto a work surface and gather gently into a ball. Wrap the dough in plastic wrap and flatten into a disk. Refrigerate at least 1 hour or overnight.

CHOCOLATE PASTRY

1 large egg yolk

2 tablespoons heavy cream

½ teaspoon vanilla extract

1½ cups all-purpose flour

6 tablespoons unsweetened Dutch-process cocoa

½ teaspoon kosher salt

½ cup granulated sugar

¾ cup (1½ sticks) plus ½ tablespoon cold unsalted butter, cut into small cubes

1. In a small bowl, stir together the egg yolk, cream, and vanilla. Set aside.

2. Sift together the flour, cocoa, and salt into a bowl of an electric mixer. Stir in the sugar. With a paddle attachment at low speed, mix the butter into the flour mixture until the mixture resembles a

coarse meal. Add the egg mixture and mix just until the dough holds together. (Do not overmix. The dough will begin to stick to the mixer paddle. It will look crumbly but feel moist.)

3. Turn the dough out onto a work surface and gather gently into a ball. Wrap the dough in plastic wrap and flatten into a disk. Refrigerate at least 1 hour or overnight.

FLAKY PIE PASTRY

3 cups all-purpose flour

¼ cup granulated sugar

1½ teaspoons kosher salt

1 cup (2 sticks) plus 2 tablespoons cold unsalted butter, cut into small cubes

¼ cup plus ½ tablespoon vegetable shortening, frozen

10 tablespoons ice water

1. In the bowl of a heavy-duty mixer, combine the flour, sugar, and salt. With a paddle attachment at low speed, mix the butter into the flour mixture until it resembles a coarse meal. Cut the frozen shortening into small cubes and add to the flour. Mix just until evenly distributed. (Larger bits of shortening should remain visible.) Gradually add the water, 1 tablespoon at a time, just until the pastry begins to come together. (The pastry will begin to stick to the paddle attachment. It will look crumbly but feel moist.)

2. Transfer the pastry to a work surface; divide in half and gather gently into 2 balls. Tightly wrap the pastry in plastic wrap and flatten each into a thick disk. Refrigerate at least 1 hour or overnight.

CORNMEAL PASTRY

1 large egg yolk

2 tablespoons heavy cream

½ teaspoon vanilla extract

¾ cup all-purpose flour

¾ cup yellow cornmeal

¼ cup granulated sugar

1 teaspoon kosher salt

½ cup (1 stick) cold unsalted butter, cut into small cubes

1. In a small bowl, stir together the egg yolk, cream, and vanilla. Set aside.

2. In a large bowl of an electric mixer, combine the flour, cornmeal, sugar, and salt. With a paddle attachment at low speed, mix the butter into the flour mixture until the mixture resembles a coarse meal. Add the egg mixture and mix just until the dough begins to hold together. (Do not overmix. The dough will begin to stick to the mixer paddle. It will look crumbly but feel moist.)

3. Turn the dough out onto a work surface and gather it gently into a ball. Wrap the dough in plastic wrap and flatten it into a disk. Refrigerate at least 1 hour or overnight.

Lining a Pan with Pastry

1. Place the pastry on a cool, lightly floured surface. Sprinkle the pastry lightly with flour. For a single pastry shell, roll the dough into a circle 1½" to 2" larger than the diameter of the pan you are using (3" to 3½" larger for an 8½" × 2" tart pan). Lift the pastry and turn it counterclockwise while rolling, to ensure even rolling and shaping as well as to prevent sticking. (Once the proper diameter is reached, the pastry should be ⅛" to ¼" thick.) Cut circles of pastry 1½" larger than the diameter of the pans. Re-roll the scraps and cut more circles if necessary.

2. Fold the pastry circle in half; place it halfway over the pan. Unfold the pastry. Lift the edge of the pastry over toward the center while pressing the pastry into the corners of the pan. Continue around the entire diameter of the pan. Press the pastry up the sides of the pan, creasing the excess pastry over the edge of the pan. Rest a rolling pin on top of the pan and roll across to cut away the excess pastry. Gently press the pastry against the side of the pan. Refrigerate the pastry shell at least 1 hour or overnight.

Baking the Pastry Shell

1. Preheat the oven as directed. Tear a piece of foil or parchment paper slightly larger than the tart or quiche pan (or use a large coffee filter). Gently press the foil or parchment into the pastry shell, turning back the edges of the foil or parchment to cover the edge of the pastry. Fill the shell halfway with pie weights or dried beans. Place the shell on a baking tray. Place the tray on the center oven rack. Bake 15 to 20 minutes or until the sides of the pastry are just set, but have not colored.

2. Carefully remove the foil and pie weights. For a partially baked crust, bake 8 to 10 minutes more for a single crust (3 to 5 minutes for individual crusts) or until the bottom of the pastry is just set. For a fully baked crust, bake 15 to 20 minutes more, or until the crust is light golden brown. (For Chocolate Pastry, bake 10 to 15 minutes more until firm when lightly pressed with a fingertip.) Cool the crust completely on a wire rack.

COCONUT-TAPIOCA TART

Wendy's love of tapioca pudding was the inspiration for this tart. When you crack through the thin sheet of caramelized sugar, the large peels of tapioca are suspended in a coconut custard that has been subtly infused with lemongrass, proving the value of fusion cuisine.

1   recipe Sweet Pastry (page 104)

Filling

1   cup milk

½   cup large pearl tapioca

1   (14-ounce) can coconut milk

¼   cup granulated sugar

1   (2") piece lemongrass, lightly smashed

¼   vanilla bean, split lengthwise

1   large egg yolk

1   tablespoon unsalted butter

¼   teaspoon kosher salt

Caramelized Topping (optional)

1½–2   tablespoons granulated sugar

1. Preheat the oven to 350°F. Line a 9½" tart pan with a removable bottom with pastry as directed (see "Lining a Pan with Pastry," page 107). Bake according to directions for a fully baked crust (see "Baking the Pastry Shell," page 107).

Filling

2. Meanwhile, in a small saucepan, heat the milk until lukewarm. Combine the warm milk and tapioca in a small bowl. Let stand to soften the tapioca, 2 hours. (Or combine cold milk and tapioca and refrigerate overnight to soften.)

3. Transfer the soaked tapioca mixture to a small saucepan; add the coconut milk, sugar, and lemongrass. Scrape out the seeds from the vanilla bean; add the seeds and the vanilla bean to the tapioca mixture. Cook the mixture over medium-low heat 20 minutes, stirring occasionally to prevent the tapioca from sticking and burning. Remove the saucepan from the heat. Remove the vanilla bean and lemongrass. Stir in the egg yolk, butter, and salt. Pour the filling into the tart crust. Refrigerate 2 hours or until the filling is set.

Caramelized Topping

4. Thirty minutes before serving, sprinkle the granulated sugar evenly over the filling. Caramelize the sugar with a blowtorch or under a preheated broiler. (If caramelizing the sugar under the broiler, it's a good idea to make a foil collar to rest over the pastry edge. This will prevent the edges from burning.) Remove the sides of the pan to serve.

Makes 1 (9½") tart, 6 to 8 servings

CHOCOLATE "MOUNDS" TART

This tart has everything in James's favorite candy bar. The pastry team of Barbara, Andrew, Stacy, and Ivette all helped to develop this recipe, a crispy chocolate pastry with a creamy coconut bottom and a baked chocolate mousse, all coated by a thin sheet of chocolate glaze. A humble candy bar turned elegant dessert!

2 recipes Chocolate Pastry (page 104)

Coconut Layer

2 cups heavy cream

1½ cups sweetened shredded coconut

1 teaspoon unsalted butter

½ teaspoon coconut extract

Chocolate Cake Layer

3½ ounces bittersweet chocolate, chopped

1 tablespoon unsalted butter, softened

2 large eggs, separated

½ teaspoon vanilla extract

2 tablespoons unsweetened Dutch-process cocoa

2 tablespoons granulated sugar

¼ cup heavy cream

¼ teaspoon kosher salt

½ cup plus 1 tablespoon warm Chocolate Glaze

1. Preheat the oven to 350°F. On a lightly floured surface, roll 1 pastry disk into a ¼"-thick round. Cut into three 5½" circles. Repeat with the second pastry disk. Line six 4" × ¾" tart pans with removable bottoms with the pastry as directed (see "Lining a Pan with Pastry," page 107). Bake according to directions for a fully baked crust (see "Baking the Pastry Shell," page 107). Reduce the oven temperature to 325°F.

Coconut Layer

2. In a small saucepan, combine the cream and coconut. Bring to a boil, stirring, over medium heat. Reduce the heat and simmer, stirring occasionally, until the cream has reduced by half and thickens, about 5 minutes. Remove the pan from the heat. Stir in the butter and coconut extract. Cool the mixture 5 minutes. Divide equally among the crusts.

3. Place the chocolate in a small bowl. Set the bowl over a saucepan halfway filled with barely simmering water. When the chocolate melts, remove the bowl from the heat and place the butter on top of the chocolate. Do not stir. In another small bowl, whisk together the egg yolks and vanilla. Pour on top of the chocolate. Do not stir. Sift the cocoa over the chocolate. Do not stir. Set aside.

4. In a small bowl of an electric mixer, beat the egg whites until soft peaks form; beat in 1 tablespoon of the sugar. In another small bowl of an electric mixer, beat the cream with the remaining 1 tablespoon sugar until soft peaks form. With a whisk, gently fold the beaten whites into the chocolate mixture just until the whites begin to incorporate. With a spatula, fold the whipped cream and salt into the chocolate just until blended. Divide the batter equally among the coconut tarts. Place the tarts on a baking tray. Bake on the center oven rack 12 minutes. (The chocolate layer should just be set. Do not overbake.) Cool the tarts on a wire rack.

5. Spoon 1½ tablespoons chocolate glaze over each tart; spread to the edges. Refrigerate the tarts 20 minutes or until the chocolate glaze is set.

Makes 6 (4") tarts

CHOCOLATE GLAZE

1 cup heavy cream

1 pound bittersweet chocolate

In a medium saucepan, bring the cream to a simmer. Remove from the heat.

Add the chocolate and stir until melted and smooth. Cool.

Makes about 3 cups

CHOCOLATE WALNUT-CARAMEL TART

James loves this rich, chocolaty smooth, and sophisticated tart. The coarse sea salt plays off the sweetness of the caramel and the bitterness of the chocolate.

1 recipe Sweet Pastry (page 104)

Walnut-Caramel Layer

½ cup granulated sugar

3 tablespoons cold water

¼ vanilla bean, split lengthwise

½ cup heavy cream

4 tablespoons unsalted butter

¼ teaspoon kosher salt

1 cup walnuts, toasted and coarsely chopped (see "Toasting Nuts," page 137)

Chocolate Ganache Layer

1 cup heavy cream

3 ounces bittersweet chocolate, chopped

1 ounce unsweetened chocolate, chopped

½ tablespoon unsalted butter, softened

2 teaspoons coarse sea salt

1. Preheat the oven to 350°F. Line a 9½" tart pan with a removable bottom with pastry as directed (see "Lining a Pan with Pastry," page 107). Bake according to directions for a fully baked crust (see "Baking the Pastry Shell," page 107).

Walnut-Caramel Layer

2. In a small saucepan, combine the sugar and water. Scrape out the seeds of the vanilla bean; stir the vanilla bean and seeds into the sugar mixture. Place the saucepan over medium-high heat; bring the sugar mixture to a boil (do not stir). As the sugar is cooking, the water will evaporate and the sugar will dissolve and begin to color. (Swirl the pan carefully and gently to ensure even cooking.) When the sugar turns a caramel color, with a long-handled spoon, quickly add the cream, butter, and salt. (The mixture will bubble vigorously.) Stir carefully to re-melt the caramel. Reduce the heat to low; remove the vanilla bean. Add the walnuts and cook until the caramel thickens, about 2 minutes. Pour the mixture into the tart crust; spread into an even layer. Refrigerate 30 minutes or until caramel has set.

Chocolate Ganache Layer

3. In a small saucepan, bring the cream to a simmer over medium heat. Remove the pan from the heat. Add the bittersweet and unsweetened chocolates; stir until melted. Add the butter and stir until smooth. Pour the ganache over the caramel layer, spreading to the edges of the tart. Refrigerate the tart 1 hour or until the ganache sets.

4. Just before serving, sprinkle the tart with the sea salt. Remove the sides of the pan.

Makes 1 (9½") tart, 6 to 8 servings

PUMPKIN CUSTARD TART WITH DATES

This creamy tart is the perfect finale to a holiday meal. Dates are the surprise ingredient, adding an exotic sweetness to the tart and complementing the flavor of the pumpkin.

---

1 recipe Sweet Pastry (page 104)

Filling

2 large eggs

1 large egg yolk

½ cup firmly packed dark brown sugar

½ cup light corn syrup

1½ cups heavy cream

1½ cups canned or fresh pumpkin puree (see "Preparing Pumpkin Puree," page 48)

1 tablespoon dark rum

1 teaspoon ground cinnamon

¾ teaspoon ground ginger

½ teaspoon kosher salt

2 cups dried dates, halved

1. Preheat the oven to 350°F. Line a large baking sheet with parchment paper. Place a 9½" × 1⅜" flan ring on the prepared sheet. Line the flan ring with pastry as directed (see "Lining a Pan with Pastry," page 107). Bake according to directions for a partially baked crust (see "Baking the Pastry Shell," page 107). Reduce the oven temperature to 325°F.

Filling

2. In a large bowl, whisk together the eggs, egg yolk, and brown sugar. Add the corn syrup and whisk until smooth. Whisk in the cream, pumpkin puree, and rum. Stir in the cinnamon, ginger, and salt.

3. Arrange the dates, cut-side down, in concentric circles over the bottom of the tart crust. Pour the pumpkin custard over the dates. Place the baking sheet on the center oven rack. Bake 25 to 30 minutes, or until the custard is just set (it should jiggle slightly in the center). Cool the tart on a wire rack 20 minutes. Remove the flan ring. Serve warm or at room temperature.

Makes 1 (9½") tart, 6 to 8 servings

CARAMELIZED APPLE TART

Caramelizing a portion of the apples intensifies this pie's apple flavor. Combined with more fresh apples, the flavors are more interesting. James also uses this filling for his apple charlotte. Be careful not to overcook the fruit, or you'll wind up with applesauce.

1 recipe Flaky Pie Pastry (page 105)

8 Granny Smith apples (or any tart, firm apple), peeled and cored

½ cup granulated sugar

¼ cup water

½ cup apple cider

1 tablespoon heavy cream

1 tablespoon brandy

1 tablespoon unsalted butter

¼ teaspoon ground cinnamon

Juice of 1 lemon

1 large egg

1 tablespoon heavy cream

1 tablespoon crystal sugar (see Resources, page 238)

1. Preheat the oven to 375°F. Line a 9½" tart pan with 1 pastry disk as directed (see "Lining a Pan with Pastry," page 107). Bake according to directions for a partially baked crust (see "Baking the Pastry Shell," page 107). Reduce the oven temperature to 350°F.

2. On a lightly floured surface, roll the remaining pastry disk into a 12" × 10" rectangle. Transfer the rectangle to a large baking sheet; refrigerate until ready to use.

3. Cut 6 of the apples into eighths. In a large sauté pan, combine the granulated sugar and water. Cook over medium heat until the sugar caramelizes to a light golden brown, about 5 minutes (do not stir). In a large sauté pan, combine the granulated sugar and water. Place the pan over medium heat; bring the sugar mixture to a boil (do not stir). As the sugar is cooking, the water will evaporate and the sugar will dissolve and begin to color. (Swirl the pan carefully and gently to ensure even cooking.) When the sugar turns a caramel color, with a long-handled spoon, quickly add the sliced apples and apple cider. (The mixture will bubble vigorously.) Stir carefully to coat the apples and re-melt the caramel. Continue to cook until the apples begin to turn translucent and the caramel is slightly reduced. Remove the pan from the heat; stir in the cream, brandy, butter, and cinnamon. Return the pan to the heat, and cook until the apples are translucent and the caramel is bubbly and slightly thickened. Cool the filling to room temperature. Cut the remaining 2 apples into eighths; stir into the filling with the lemon juice.

4. Whisk the egg and the cream together in a small bowl. Spread the apple filling in the crust; brush the edges of the crust with the egg wash. With a fluted pastry wheel, cut the pastry rectangle into ten 1"-wide strips. Arrange 5 strips equidistant over the filling. Place the remaining 5 strips at a 45° angle over the top, to create a lattice pattern. Secure the ends of the strips to the crust; trim the overhang. Brush the lattice with the egg wash and sprinkle with the crystal sugar. Refrigerate the tart 15 minutes.

5. Bake on the center oven rack 45 to 50 minutes, or until the center of the filling is bubbly. Cool the tart in the pan on a wire rack 30 minutes. Carefully remove the sides of the pan and cool completely.

Makes 1 (9") tart

FIG AND ALMOND TART

In this tart, as the figs bake, they release their sweet juices and blend with the almond cream, producing an extraordinary flavor further enhanced by a crunchy cornmeal crust.

---

1 recipe Cornmeal Pastry (page 106)

2 tablespoons unsalted butter

¼ vanilla bean

¼ cup plain yogurt

1 large egg

2 tablespoons granulated sugar

⅓ cup whole blanched almonds, toasted and finely ground (see "Toasting Nuts," page 137)

1 tablespoon all-purpose flour

1½ teaspoons almond extract

⅛ teaspoon kosher salt

18–20 fresh figs, stems removed

Confectioners' sugar

1. Preheat the oven to 350°F. Line a 9½" tart pan with a removable bottom with pastry as directed (see "Lining a Pan with Pastry," page 107). Bake according to directions for a partially baked crust (see "Baking the Pastry Shell," page 107). Leave the oven on.

2. In a small saucepan, melt the butter and vanilla bean over medium heat. Cook until the butter bubbles and turns golden brown. Quickly pour browned butter through a fine mesh strainer into a small bowl; remove the vanilla bean. Cool. Whisk in the yogurt, egg, sugar, almonds, flour, extract, and salt. Spread filling over the bottom of the crust.

3. Cut the figs in half. Arrange the halves, close together and cut side up, in concentric circles over the filling.

4. Place the tart on a baking tray; place the tray on the center oven rack. Bake 40 to 45 minutes, or until the filling is golden brown and the figs release their juices. Cool the tart on a wire rack 15 minutes; remove the sides of the pan. Dust the top with confectioners' sugar. Serve warm or at room temperature.

Makes 1 (9½") tart, 6 to 8 servings

PLUM AND BLACKBERRY CRISPS

The sweet and tart fruit is the perfect foil for the buttery crisp crumb topping in this recipe. Plum and blackberry crisps are particularly delicious served with vanilla or cinnamon ice cream or with whipped heavy cream.

1½ recipes Sweet Pastry (page 104)

Topping

1½ cups plus 2 tablespoons all-purpose flour

½ cup firmly packed dark brown sugar

½ cup granulated sugar

½ teaspoon kosher salt

⅛ teaspoon baking powder

¾ cup (1½ sticks) unsalted butter, melted and cooled slightly

Filling

½ cup granulated sugar

¼ cup water

6 plums, sliced in eighths

1 teaspoon unsalted butter

1½ cups fresh blackberries

Grated zest of 1 lime

2 tablespoons cornstarch

2 tablespoons fresh lime juice

1. Preheat the oven to 350°F. Line six 3" × 1¼" tart pans with removable bottoms with pastry as directed (see "Lining a Pan with Pastry," page 107). Bake according to directions for a partially baked crust (see "Baking the Pastry Shell," page 107). Leave the oven on.

Topping

2. In a small bowl, toss together the flour, brown and granulated sugars, salt, and baking powder. Add melted butter and toss until the flour is moistened and crumbly. Refrigerate the crumbs until firm, 15 minutes.

Filling

3. Meanwhile, in a medium sauté pan, combine the granulated sugar and water. Place the pan over medium-high heat; bring the sugar mixture to a boil (do not stir). As the sugar is cooking the water will evaporate and the sugar will dissolve and begin to color. (Swirl the pan carefully and gently to ensure even cooking.) Continue to cook until the sugar caramelizes, about 3 minutes. Quickly add the plums; toss to coat with the caramel. Reduce the heat and cook until the caramel re-melts and plums release their juices. Add the butter and cook until the syrup is slightly reduced, 3 minutes. Add blackberries and lime zest. Cook 2 minutes. Meanwhile, in a small cup, dissolve the cornstarch in the lime juice. Remove the pan from the heat; stir in the dissolved cornstarch. Cool.

4. Line a large baking tray with parchment paper. Divide the filling evenly among the tart crusts. Sprinkle the topping evenly over the tops. Place the crisps on the prepared tray; place the tray on the center oven rack. Bake 25 to 30 minutes, until the topping is golden and the filling is bubbly around the edges. Cool the crisps on a wire rack. Remove the sides of the pans.

Makes 6 (3") crisps

TOP-CRUST BLUEBERRY PIES

Even the most experienced cooks, for some reason, are intimidated by the idea of a perfect piecrust. This recipe saves you the trouble of lining a pie plate. By making a simple biscuit dough topped with fruit and covered by a round of flaky pastry, you achieve the same result.

1 recipe Flaky Pie Pastry (page 105)

Biscuit Dough

¼ cup plus 2 tablespoons all-purpose flour

2 teaspoons granulated sugar

¾ teaspoon baking powder

¼ teaspoon kosher salt

1 tablespoon unsalted butter

2 tablespoons heavy cream

Fruit Filling

6 cups fresh blueberries

½ cup granulated sugar

2 tablespoons cornstarch

Juice and grated zest of 1 lemon

½ teaspoon ground cinnamon

6 teaspoons butter

1 large egg

1 teaspoon heavy cream

1. On a lightly floured surface, roll 1 pastry disk into a ¼"-thick round. Cut into three 5" circles. Transfer the circles to a baking sheet. Repeat process with the remaining pastry disk. Refrigerate the circles until ready to use.

Biscuit Dough

2. In a small bowl, stir together the flour, sugar, baking powder, and salt. With a pastry blender or 2 knives, cut the butter into the flour until the mixture resembles a coarse meal. Add the cream and mix until it forms a dough. Press 1½ tablespoons dough over the bottom of each of six 4½" × 1½" ramekins. Set aside.

Fruit Filling

3. In a large bowl, toss the blueberries with the sugar, cornstarch, lemon juice and zest, and cinnamon. Divide the filling among the 6 ramekins; dot the top of each with 1 teaspoon butter.

4. Place a pastry circle over each ramekin. Crimp the edges of the pastry to the sides of each ramekin. In small bowl, whisk together the egg and cream. Brush the pastry with the egg wash. Cut a small hole in the center of each to create a vent for the steam to escape. (You may decorate the tops of each pie with leaves and vines made from pastry scraps.) Place the pies on a baking tray. Refrigerate 30 minutes.

5. Meanwhile, preheat the oven to 350°F. Place the tray with the pies on the center oven rack. Bake about 45 minutes, until the pastry is golden brown and the juices begin to bubble. Cool the pies on a wire rack.

Makes 6 (4½") pies

STRAWBERRY-RHUBARB PIE

This recipe was created by our former pastry chef Barbara Bonett, who was with Metropolitan from the early days. Her uncle loves this pie so much that he demands she bring it every time she visits him.

1 recipe Flaky Pie Pastry (page 105)

½ cup granulated sugar

2 tablespoons water

¾ pound rhubarb, trimmed and cut into 1" pieces (4 cups)

2 tablespoons unsalted butter

2 cups strawberries, hulled and cut in half

¼ cup orange juice

2 tablespoons cornstarch

1½ tablespoons grated orange zest

¼ teaspoon kosher salt

⅛ teaspoon ground cinnamon

1 large egg

1 teaspoon heavy cream

1 teaspoon crystal sugar (see Resources, page 238)

1. Preheat the oven to 375°F. Line an 8½" × 2" tart pan with a removable bottom with 1 pastry disk as directed (see "Lining a Pan with Pastry," page 107). Bake according to directions for a partially baked crust (see "Baking the Pastry Shell," page 107). Reduce the oven temperature to 350°F.

2. On a lightly floured surface, roll remaining pastry disk into an 8" × 10" rectangle. Transfer the rectangle to a large baking sheet; refrigerate until ready to use.

3. In a large sauté pan, bring the sugar and water to a boil over medium-high heat. Cook the syrup 1 minute. Stir in the rhubarb and butter. Cook just until rhubarb is tender, 3 minutes. Transfer the rhubarb to a bowl and cool.

4. In a large bowl, toss together the strawberries, orange juice, cornstarch, orange zest, salt, and cinnamon. Fold in the cooled rhubarb. Pour the filling into the crust. Set aside.

5. Line a large baking tray with parchment paper. In a small bowl, whisk together the egg and heavy cream.

6. With a fluted pastry wheel, cut the pastry rectangle into eight 1"-thick strips. Lightly brush the edges of the pastry with the egg wash. Place 4 strips equidistant over the pie. Brush the strips lightly with the egg wash. Place the remaining 4 strips at a 45-degree angle over the top to create a lattice pattern. Brush with the egg wash. Secure the ends of the strips to the crust; trim the overhang. Sprinkle the pie with the crystal sugar. Place the pie on the prepared baking tray. Place the tray on the center oven rack. Bake 45 to 50 minutes, until golden brown and juices are bubbling. Cool completely on a wire rack.

Makes 1 (8½") pie, 6 to 8 servings

SAVORY CHEESE AND LEEK TART

Dan Grimes—who owns Chloe Restaurant in Philadelphia with his wife, Maryanne—was one of Metropolitan's first associates. He contributed this recipe in honor of the hand pies and small savory tarts he always made at the bakery. The richness of the ricotta and goat cheeses in this tart combines beautifully with the sweet sautéed leeks.

4 tablespoons unsalted butter

3 leeks (white part only), cleaned and cut into 1" pieces

3 cups ricotta cheese

¾ cup freshly grated Parmesan cheese

4 ounces goat cheese

2 large eggs

2 tablespoons chopped fresh thyme

Salt and freshly ground black pepper to taste

1 cup fresh bread crumbs

2 tablespoons chopped flat-leaf parsley

½ recipe Flaky Pie Pastry (page 105)

2 tablespoons Dijon mustard

2 tablespoons heavy cream

2 teaspoons black sesame seeds

2 teaspoons white sesame seeds

1. Preheat the oven to 450°F. In a large sauté pan, melt 2 tablespoons of the butter over medium heat. Add the leeks and cook until tender, about 5 minutes. Set aside to cool.

2. In a large bowl, stir together the ricotta, ½ cup of the Parmesan, and the goat cheese. Stir in the eggs, thyme, salt, and pepper.

3. In a small bowl, toss together the bread crumbs, the remaining ¼ cup Parmesan, and the parsley. Melt the remaining 2 tablespoons butter; stir into the bread crumb mixture until evenly moistened.

4. Line a large baking sheet with parchment paper. On a lightly floured surface, roll the pastry into a 12" circle. Transfer the pastry circle to the prepared sheet.

5. Brush the mustard over the pastry, leaving a 3" border. Spread the leeks evenly over the mustard. Top the leeks with the cheese mixture, still leaving the 3" border. Sprinkle the bread crumb mixture over the cheese. Starting at 1 point of the circle, fold the edge of the pastry over the filling, forming a pleated border. Brush the pastry border with the cream; sprinkle with the sesame seeds. Bake the tart 15 minutes. Reduce the oven temperature to 375°F. Bake 40 minutes more, or until golden brown. Serve warm or at room temperature.

Makes 1 (9") tart, 6 servings

Summer Tomato and Fresh Mozzarella Tart

If you grow your own tomatoes and suddenly find yourself with an abundant harvest of fruit, as most of us do, this tart will make great use of your excess!

½ recipe Flaky Pie Pastry (page 105)

½ cup Basil Pesto (page 222)

¾ cup fresh bread crumbs

6 tomatoes (preferably organic and local), cut into ¼"-thick slices

4 (4-ounce) fresh mozzarella balls (preferably *mozzarella di bufala*), sliced thick

4 tablespoons freshly grated Pecorino Romano cheese

1 bunch fresh basil leaves, washed, dried, and torn

1 tablespoon kosher salt

½ teaspoon cracked black pepper

2 tablespoons balsamic vinegar

5 tablespoons extra-virgin olive oil

1 large egg

1 tablespoon heavy cream

¼ cup pine nuts, finely ground

1. Preheat the oven to 400°F. Line a large baking sheet with parchment paper.

2. On a lightly floured surface, roll the pastry into a 12" circle. Transfer the pastry circle to the prepared sheet. Spread the pesto over the pastry, leaving a 2" border. Sprinkle ½ cup of the bread crumbs over the pesto. Alternately arrange half the tomato and mozzarella slices, overlapping slightly in concentric circles. Sprinkle the top with 2 tablespoons of the Pecorino, half the basil, ½ tablespoon of the salt, ¼ teaspoon of the pepper, 1 tablespoon of the vinegar, and 2 tablespoons of the oil. Repeat with a second layer of the remaining tomatoes and mozzarella, the 2 tablespoons Pecorino, the remaining basil, the ½ tablespoon salt, ¼ teaspoon pepper, 1 tablespoon vinegar, and 2 tablespoons of the oil.

3. Starting at 1 point of the circle, fold the edge of the pastry over the filling, forming a pleated border. In a small bowl, whisk together the egg and cream; brush on the pastry border. In a small bowl, toss together the remaining ¼ cup bread crumbs, the pine nuts, and the remaining 1 tablespoon oil. Sprinkle the mixture over the tart. Bake the tart 35 to 40 minutes, or until golden brown. Serve warm or at room temperature.

Makes 1 (10") tart, 6 to 8 servings

ASPARAGUS, HAM, AND PARSLEY QUICHE

This recipe utilizes the classic quiche ingredients of Gruyère cheese and smoked ham. It is best made in the spring when the most flavorful asparagus are plentiful.

½ recipe Flaky Pie Pastry (page 105)

Custard

1¼ cups heavy cream

¾ cup milk

4 large egg yolks

2 large eggs

1 teaspoon kosher salt

¼ teaspoon freshly ground black pepper

Filling

12 asparagus spears, ends trimmed

1 teaspoon extra-virgin olive oil

1 teaspoon fresh lemon juice

Pinch of salt

Pinch of freshly ground black pepper

1 cup diced smoked ham

½ cup coarsely chopped flat-leaf parsley

2 cups shredded Gruyère cheese

1. Preheat the oven to 375°F. Line an 8½" × 2" tart pan with a removable bottom with pastry as directed (see "Lining a Pan with Pastry," page 107). Bake according to directions for a partially baked crust (see "Baking the Pastry Shell," page 107). Leave the oven on.

Custard

2. In a bowl, whisk together the cream, milk, egg yolks, eggs, salt, and pepper. Set aside.

Filling

3. On a baking tray, toss together the asparagus, oil, lemon juice, salt, and pepper. Spread the asparagus in an even layer. Roast 8 minutes at 375°F or until tender. Cool. Slice the asparagus into ½" pieces; toss in a bowl with the ham. Spread the asparagus and ham in the crust. Sprinkle the top with the parsley, then the Gruyère.

4. Reduce the oven temperature to 325°F. Line a large baking tray with parchment paper. Place the tart pan on the prepared tray. Gently pour the custard over the filling. Place the tray on the center oven rack. Bake about 45 minutes, until the custard is set and the top is light golden brown. Cool on a wire rack. Remove the sides of the pan.

Makes 1 quiche, 8 to 10 servings

VEGETABLE QUICHE

This retro food has earned its place among the classics.

½ recipe Flaky Pie Pastry (page 105)

Custard

2 cups Crème Fraîche

4 large eggs

4 large egg yolks

1 teaspoon kosher salt

¼ teaspoon freshly ground black pepper

⅛ teaspoon freshly grated nutmeg

Vegetables

2 tablespoons olive oil

1 teaspoon garlic, minced

4 bunches fresh spinach, stems removed, washed, and dried (see "Washing Leafy Greens," page 207)

1 teaspoon fresh lemon juice

¼ teaspoon kosher salt

⅛ teaspoon freshly ground black pepper

1 large roasted red bell pepper, diced (see "Roasting Peppers," page 217)

2 cups shredded Fontina cheese

1 tablespoon chopped fresh basil

1 tablespoon coarsely chopped flat-leaf parsley

½ tablespoon freshly grated Parmesan cheese

1. Preheat the oven to 375°F. Line an 8½" × 2" tart pan with a removable bottom with pastry as directed (see "Lining a Pan with Pastry," page 107). Bake according to directions for a partially baked crust (see "Baking the Pastry Shell," page 107). Reduce the oven temperature to 325°F.

Custard

2. In a large bowl, whisk together the crème fraîche, eggs, egg yolks, salt, pepper, and nutmeg until smooth. Set aside.

Vegetables

3. In a large sauté pan, heat the oil over medium heat. Add the garlic and sauté 1 minute. Add the spinach, lemon juice, salt, and pepper. Cook until the spinach is wilted, about 3 minutes. Drain the spinach; cool.

4. Line a large baking tray with parchment paper. Spread the cooled spinach over the bottom of the crust. Distribute the roasted pepper evenly over the top. Sprinkle the Fontina, basil, and parsley over the vegetables. Place the tart pan on the prepared tray. Carefully pour the custard over the vegetables. Sprinkle the top of the custard with the Parmesan. Place the tray on the center oven rack. Bake 40 to 45 minutes, until the custard is set. Cool completely on a wire rack. Remove the sides of the pan.

Makes 1 (8¹⁄₂") quiche, 8 to 10 servings

CRÈME FRAÎCHE

Crème fraîche can replace heavy cream in most recipes where you would prefer its fresh tangy flavor.

3 cups heavy cream

1 cup buttermilk

In a bowl, whisk together the cream and buttermilk; pour into a clean jar. Cover and let stand at room temperature 24 hours.

Uncover the jar and whisk the cream. It should be noticeably thicker. (If not, cover and let stand another 8 hours. Continue to check up to 48 hours.) Refrigerate the crème fraîche 24 hours, then use as desired.

Makes 1 quart

Variations:

Try adding 2 vanilla beans, split lengthwise and scraped, to the cream and buttermilk for vanilla-flavored crème fraîche. Or, combine 1 cup of the cream and a cinnamon stick in a saucepan; warm slightly. Refrigerate until chilled. Stir into the remaining cream and buttermilk, and proceed as directed.

Cookies and
Cookie Bars

Cookies and cookie bars are an ideal confection. They soothe and satisfy without a hint of pretension—the perfect little ending to a meal or the perfect beginning. Mastering a few basic techniques enables even a novice baker to create variations in style and flavor. For many of the following recipes, the dough can be frozen and then baked as an impromptu dessert for unexpected guests. Any of the recipes can be modified to produce smaller or larger cookies. When planning to serve a cookie assortment, consider varying sizes, shapes, and textures as well as flavors.

OATMEAL-RAISIN COOKIES

*Crunchy, chewy, and moist, these oat-filled cookies are a great
snack to pull you through the midday slump.*

¾ cup plus 1 teaspoon all-purpose
flour

1 teaspoon ground cinnamon

1 teaspoon kosher salt

½ teaspoon baking soda

1⅔ cups old-fashioned oats

¾ cup (1½ sticks) unsalted butter,
softened

2⅓ cups firmly packed dark brown sugar

½ cup plus 2 tablespoons granulated
sugar

1 large egg

1 tablespoon vanilla extract

1¼ cups dark raisins

½ cup pecans, toasted and coarsely
chopped (see "Toasting Nuts")

1. Preheat the oven to 350°F. Line 2 large baking sheets with parchment paper or use nonstick baking sheets.

2. In a large bowl, combine the flour, cinnamon, salt, baking soda, and oats. In a large bowl of an electric mixer, beat the butter, brown and granulated sugars until light and fluffy. Beat in the egg, then the vanilla. At low speed, stir in the flour mixture just until combined. Fold in the raisins and pecans.

3. Drop the dough by 2-tablespoon portions, 2" apart, on the prepared baking sheets. Bake 15 to 20 minutes, rotating the baking sheets between the upper and lower oven racks halfway through baking, until light golden brown. Transfer the cookies to wire racks to cool completely. Repeat with the remaining dough.

Makes 2 dozen cookies

TOASTING NUTS

Toasting nuts releases their natural oils. If toasted too long, nuts become bitter, so it is best to toast lightly to bring out a robust, nutty flavor. To toast, preheat the oven to 325°F. Spread nuts evenly on a baking sheet. Bake on the center oven rack for 10 to 12 minutes, or until fragrant and toasted. Cool.

CHOCOLATE CHIP COOKIES

When James was the pastry chef at the White Dog Café, he experimented with every kind of chocolate chip cookie—thin and crispy, thick and chewy, nuts, no nuts—until he came up with the perfect cookie. The secret is grinding the oats into flour, which adds a slight nuttiness and crunch that is absolutely addicting.

1½ cups old-fashioned oats

3 cups all-purpose flour, sifted

1½ teaspoons baking powder

1½ teaspoons baking soda

¾ teaspoon kosher salt

1 cup milk chocolate chunks

1½ cups (3 sticks) unsalted butter, softened

1½ cups granulated sugar

1½ cups firmly packed dark brown sugar

3 large eggs

1½ teaspoons vanilla extract

3 cups bittersweet chocolate chunks

1½ cups pecans, toasted and coarsely chopped (see "Toasting Nuts," page 137)

1½ cups walnuts, toasted and coarsely chopped (see "Toasting Nuts," page 137)

1. Preheat the oven to 350°F. Line 2 large baking sheets with parchment paper or use nonstick baking sheets.

2. In a food processor, grind the oats until they become a fine flour. In a large bowl, combine the ground oats, flour, baking powder, baking soda, and salt. Using the small holes of a box grater, grate the milk chocolate; stir into the flour mixture. Set aside.

3. In a large bowl of an electric mixer, beat the butter until creamy. Add the granulated and brown sugars, and beat until light and fluffy. Add the eggs, one at a time, beating

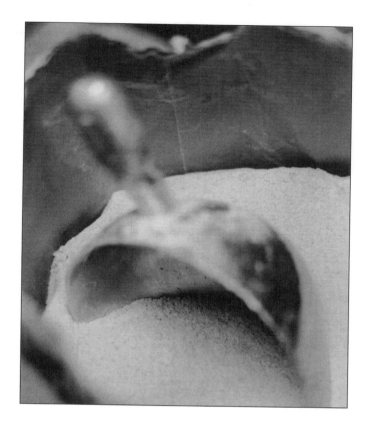

after each addition. Beat in the vanilla. At low speed, stir in the flour mixture just until combined. Fold in the chocolate chunks, pecans, and walnuts.

4. Drop the dough by 2-tablespoon portions (use 2 teaspoons for smaller cookies), 2" apart, on the prepared baking sheets. Bake 15 to 20 minutes, rotating the baking sheets between the upper and lower oven racks halfway through baking, until light golden brown. Transfer the cookies to wire racks to cool completely. Repeat with the remaining dough.

Makes 2 dozen large cookies or 4 dozen small cookies

PIROUETTES

These elegant little cookies can be found in various shapes and forms. They may be left unshaped and cooked into thin round cookies or they may be shaped into fanciful small ice cream cones. The success of these fragile cookies depends on all of the ingredients being at room temperature when they are being utilized.

¾ cup (1½ sticks) plus 5 tablespoons unsalted butter, softened

¾ cup plus 1 tablespoon confectioners' sugar

5 large egg whites, at room temperature

1 teaspoon vanilla extract

1 cup all-purpose flour, sifted

½ cup whole blanched almonds, finely ground

½ cup coarsely chopped bittersweet chocolate

Grated zest of 2 lemons

1 teaspoon kosher salt

1. Preheat the oven to 425°F.

2. In a large bowl of an electric mixer, beat the butter until creamy. Add the confectioners' sugar and beat until light and fluffy. Add the egg whites, one at a time, beating after each addition. Beat in the vanilla. Gently stir in the flour, almonds, chocolate, lemon zest, and salt (do not overmix).

3. Drop the batter by heaping tablespoons, 6" apart, on 2 large nonstick baking sheets, making only 4 cookies per sheet. Bake 1 sheet at a time on the center oven rack, 8 to 10 minutes, or until golden brown around the edges. Working quickly, remove 1 cookie with a thin, flexible spatula and place, bottom-side up, on the counter. Immediately wrap the hot cookie around a 1"-thick metal or wooden dowel. Cool completely on a wire rack. (The cookies will become very crisp as they cool.) Repeat with the remaining cookies. (If cookies harden before being wrapped around the dowel, return to oven 1 minute to soften, then wrap.)

Tip: Wooden dowels can be purchased in a hardware store. It is best to use a dowel approximately 12" long. The ends of a wooden spoon may also be substituted.

Makes 3 dozen cookies

GINGER THINS

These elegant, thin, spicy wafers are reminiscent of the Moravian Christmas cookie. For a chewy cookie, bake for no more than 12 minutes. For a crisper cookie, bake for 15 minutes.

2⅓ cups all-purpose flour	¾ cup granulated sugar
2 teaspoons baking soda	¾ cup firmly packed dark brown sugar
2 teaspoons ground ginger	1 teaspoon grated fresh gingerroot
½ teaspoon ground cloves	1 large egg
½ teaspoon kosher salt	½ teaspoon vanilla extract
1 cup (2 sticks) unsalted butter	⅓ cup dark molasses

1. Preheat the oven to 325°F. Line 2 large baking sheets with parchment paper or use nonstick baking sheets.

2. In a large bowl, sift together the flour, baking soda, ground ginger, cloves, and salt. In a large bowl of an electric mixer, beat the butter, granulated and brown sugars, and gingerroot until light and fluffy. Beat in the egg and the vanilla. Add the molasses and beat well. At low speed, add the flour mixture and stir until well combined.

3. For each cookie, scoop a tablespoon of dough and round into a ball between moistened hands. Arrange the balls, 2" apart, on the prepared baking sheets. Flatten the cookies slightly with the bottom of a glass dipped in warm water. Bake 10 to 12 minutes, or until golden brown. Transfer the cookies to wire racks to cool completely. Repeat with the remaining dough.

Makes 3 dozen cookies

LEMON-THYME CRISPS

Fresh ginger in these rich, crisp biscuits brightens the lemon-thyme flavor in these addictive cookies. This recipe comes to us from Anne Marie Lasher, an old friend and colleague from our White Dog Café days. Anne Marie now owns Picnic, a terrific take-out establishment in West Philadelphia.

3¼ cups all-purpose flour

2 teaspoons baking powder

½ teaspoon kosher salt

1 cup (2 sticks) unsalted butter, softened

1½ cups granulated sugar

Juice and grated zest of 1 lemon

2 tablespoons minced fresh ginger

2 tablespoons chopped fresh lemon thyme

1 large egg

1. In a large bowl, sift together the flour, baking powder, and salt. Set aside.

2. In a large bowl of an electric mixer, beat the butter and sugar until light and fluffy. Add the lemon juice and zest, ginger, and thyme; beat well. Beat in the egg. At low speed, stir in the flour mixture just until combined.

3. Divide the dough into 4 pieces. Roll each piece into a 2"-diameter log. Wrap each log in plastic wrap or parchment paper and refrigerate overnight (or up to a week).

4. Preheat the oven to 325°F. Line 2 large baking sheets with parchment paper or use nonstick baking sheets. On the bias, cut each log into ¼"-thick slices. Place the slices, 1" apart, on the prepared baking sheets. Bake about 15 minutes, rotating the baking sheets between the upper and lower oven racks halfway through baking, until golden brown on the edges.

MAKES 5 DOZEN COOKIES

SESAME COOKIES

These cookies are our adaptation of a recipe by our friend Nicole Routhier, from her book, The Foods of Vietnam.

½ cup plus 1 tablespoon sesame seeds

1½ cups plus 2 tablespoons all-purpose flour

¾ teaspoon baking powder

½ teaspoon baking soda

¼ teaspoon kosher salt

1 large egg

1 teaspoon vanilla extract

1 teaspoon toasted sesame oil

1 cup (2 sticks) plus 1 tablespoon butter, softened

¾ cup granulated sugar

1 large egg white, lightly beaten (for brushing)

1. Preheat the oven to 325°F. Lightly butter 2 large baking sheets.

2. Spread the sesame seeds on another baking sheet. Bake 10 minutes or until golden. Cool completely. Remove 1 tablespoon of the sesame seeds for the garnish; set aside. Transfer the remaining sesame seeds to a food processor; grind the seeds to a powder.

3. In a small bowl, stir together the ground sesame seeds, flour, baking powder, baking soda, and salt. In another small bowl, stir together the egg, vanilla, and sesame oil.

4. In a large bowl of an electric mixer, beat the butter until creamy. Add the sugar and beat until light and fluffy. At low speed, add the flour mixture, alternately with the egg mixture, beginning and ending with the flour mixture, just until blended.

5. Drop the dough by rounded tablespoons, 2" apart, on the prepared baking sheets. Flatten the cookies with the bottom of a glass lightly dipped in hot water. Brush the tops with the egg white; sprinkle with the reserved sesame seeds.

6. Bake 18 to 20 minutes, rotating the baking sheets between the upper and lower oven racks halfway through baking, until light golden brown. Transfer the cookies to wire racks to cool completely. Repeat with the remaining dough.

Makes 2 dozen cookies

CHOCOLATE-DIPPED ORANGE PECAN SHORTBREAD

This chocolate-dipped cookie is an elegant dressed-up version of an excellent shortbread dough. Made without the orange zest, orange oil, and pecans, it becomes a classic shortbread cookie. Add lavender and honey, and it is transformed once again. Let the basic recipe inspire you to create your own variations.

Cookie Dough

1½ cups (3 sticks) unsalted butter

¾ cup firmly packed dark brown sugar

Grated zest of 1 orange

1 teaspoon vanilla extract

½ teaspoon pure orange oil (such as Boyajian; see Resources, page 238)

3 cups all-purpose flour

1 cup pecans, toasted and coarsely chopped (see "Toasting Nuts," page 137)

¾ teaspoon kosher salt

Chocolate Glaze

8 ounces bittersweet chocolate, chopped

1 tablespoon canola oil

Cookie Dough

1. Line three 3½" × 6" mini loaf pans with plastic wrap. In a large bowl of an electric mixer, beat the butter until creamy. Add the sugar, orange zest, vanilla, and orange oil; beat until light and fluffy. At low speed, stir in the flour, pecans, and salt until combined. Divide the dough between the prepared loaf pans; press evenly into the bottom of each pan, making sure the corners are filled. Fold the plastic wrap over the dough. Working 1 pan at a time, place a baking tray on top of each pan. Press down firmly on the tray so the dough in the pan is evenly distributed among all 4 corners and there are no air pockets. Freeze the dough 4 hours or overnight, until firm.

2. Preheat the oven to 325°F. Line 2 large baking sheets with parchment paper or use nonstick baking sheets.

3. Unmold the dough from the pans; remove the plastic wrap. With a knife dipped in hot water, cut each piece of dough into twelve ⅛"-thick rectangles. Place the shortbread, 1" apart, on the prepared baking sheets. Bake 12 to 15 minutes, rotating the baking sheets between the upper and lower oven racks halfway through baking, until light golden brown around the edges. Transfer the shortbread to wire racks to cool completely.

Chocolate Glaze

4. Line a baking sheet with parchment paper. In a heatproof bowl, combine the chocolate and the oil. Set the bowl over a saucepan filled with 1" of simmering water. Heat, stirring occasionally, until the chocolate melts and the glaze is smooth. Remove the bowl from the heat. Dip each shortbread halfway into the glaze and place on the prepared baking sheet. Let the shortbread stand until the glaze sets.

Makes 3 dozen shortbread

CHOCOLATE BISCOTTI

Although in Italy, biscotti *is the term for cookie, here is a recipe that has become synonymous with the name biscotti. They are a wonderful dipping cookie or accompaniment to ice cream or sorbet.*

---

3 cups plus 2 tablespoons all-purpose flour

½ cup unsweetened cocoa

2¼ teaspoons baking powder

1 teaspoon kosher salt

¾ cup (1½ sticks) unsalted butter

1¾ cups granulated sugar

4 large eggs

Grated zest of 1 lemon

2 tablespoons coffee liqueur

1 cup bittersweet chocolate chunks

1 cup whole blanched almonds, toasted (see "Toasting Nuts," page 137)

1. Preheat the oven to 325°F. Line 2 large baking sheets with parchment paper or use nonstick baking sheets.

2. In a large bowl, sift together the flour, cocoa, baking powder, and salt. In a large bowl of an electric mixer, beat the butter and 1¼ cups sugar until light and fluffy. Beat in the eggs, one at a time, then add the lemon zest and liqueur. At low speed, add the flour mixture just until combined. Stir in the chocolate chunks and almonds.

3. Sprinkle a work surface with the remaining ½ cup sugar. Divide the dough in half. Roll each piece in the sugar into a 15" log. Arrange the logs, 3" apart, on 1 prepared baking sheet. Bake for 30 minutes or until center of each log is firm when gently pressed with a fingertip. Cool logs on the baking sheet 1 hour or overnight.

4. Preheat the oven to 300°F. Transfer the logs to a large cutting board. With a serrated knife, slice each log crosswise into ¼"-thick slices. Transfer the slices, cut-side down, to the baking sheets. Bake 12 to15 minutes until crisp. Transfer the biscotti to wire racks and cool completely.

Make 3½ dozen biscotti

LEMON BARS

Our lemon bars are a wonderful combination of sweet and tart.
The crisp, buttery crust complements the tart filling.

Crust

1½ cups (3 sticks) cold unsalted
    butter

¾ cup granulated sugar

1 large egg yolk

1 teaspoon vanilla extract

3 cups all-purpose flour

¾ teaspoon kosher salt

Custard Filling

4 cups granulated sugar

  Grated zest of 3 lemons

½ cup plus 1 tablespoon all-purpose
   flour

¼ teaspoon kosher salt

1¾ cups fresh lemon juice

12 large eggs

3 tablespoons confectioners' sugar

1. In the bowl of a heavy-duty mixer with a paddle attachment, beat the butter until creamy. Add the granulated sugar and beat until light and fluffy. Beat in the egg yolk and vanilla. At low speed, add the flour and salt and mix just until combined. Shape dough into disk; wrap in plastic wrap and refrigerate 20 minutes.

2. Preheat the oven to 350°F. Butter a 17" × 11" × 1" baking pan.

3. On a lightly floured surface, roll out the dough to a 17" × 11" rectangle. Carefully roll up the dough around the rolling pin. Lift the rolling pin over 1 short end of the prepared baking pan, then unravel the dough so that it covers the pan. Press the dough into the corners and up the sides of the pan. Refrigerate for 20 minutes.

4. Bake the crust 15 minutes or until light golden brown.

Custard Filling

5. Combine 1 cup of the granulated sugar and the lemon zest in a food processor; process until the sugar becomes infused with the lemon, about 30 seconds. Pour the sugar into a large bowl. Add the remaining 3 cups granulated sugar, flour, and salt, stirring well (this will help avoid lumps of flour in the filling). Whisk in the lemon juice until the mixture is smooth, then whisk in the eggs until blended. Pour the topping evenly over the crust. Bake on the center oven rack 22 to 25 minutes, or until the topping is set. Cool completely on a wire rack. Cut into 24 bars, then sprinkle lightly with the confectioners' sugar.

Makes 2 dozen bars

DATE-WALNUT BARS

This recipe spotlights the underutilized, often maligned date. Dates are a great source of protein and iron, making this a satisfying choice for a breakfast bar. For those who are not date lovers, high-quality raspberry preserves may be substituted for the date filling.

Filling

¾	pound Medjool dates
1½	cups water
1	tablespoon unsalted butter
	Grated zest of 1 orange
1	teaspoon ground cinnamon

Crust

2	cups walnuts, toasted (see "Toasting Nuts," page 137)
3	cups all-purpose flour
1	cup granulated sugar
1	teaspoon kosher salt
1	cup (2 sticks) plus 2 tablespoons cold unsalted butter, cut into cubes
1	large egg, lightly beaten

1. In a medium saucepan, combine the dates, water, butter, orange zest, and cinnamon. Bring to a simmer over medium-low heat. Simmer 5 minutes or until the dates are soft and the butter is melted. Remove the pan from the heat and cool 5 minutes. Transfer the filling to a food processor; pulse until dates are roughly chopped. Set aside.

2. Preheat the oven to 325°F. Butter a 13" × 9" baking pan.

Crust

3. In a food processor, process the walnuts until finely ground. Transfer the nuts to a large bowl, stir in the flour, sugar, and salt. Toss the butter into the flour mixture. With a pastry blender or 2 knives, cut in the butter until the mixture is crumbly. Add the egg and lightly toss just until blended (so the mixture remains crumbly).

4. Press two-thirds of the crust into the prepared baking pan. Spread the filling evenly over the crust, then sprinkle the remaining one-third of the crumbled crust over the filling. Bake on the center oven rack 35 to 40 minutes or until golden brown. Cool completely on a wire rack. Cut into 20 bars.

Makes 20 bars

FIG BARS

After long days as a young pastry chef, James's favorite snack was a fig bar made at a tiny bakeshop in Philadelphia owned by Grace Kelly's niece. That shop has long since closed, so to satisfy his fig bar craving, we had to develop our own version.

Dough

- 2½ cups all-purpose flour
- ¼ teaspoon baking soda
- ¼ teaspoon ground cinnamon
- ¼ teaspoon kosher salt
- ½ cup (1 stick) plus 2 tablespoons unsalted butter
- ½ cup firmly packed dark brown sugar
- 1 large egg
- 1 large egg yolk
- 1 teaspoon vanilla extract

Filling

- 2 cups dried Black Mission figs, stems removed
- 1 cup water
- ½ cup raspberry preserves
- Juice and grated zest of 1 lemon

Glaze

- 1 large egg
- 1 teaspoon milk
- 2 tablespoons crystal sugar (see Resources, page 238)

Dough

1. In a large bowl, sift together the flour, baking soda, cinnamon, and salt. In the bowl of a heavy-duty mixer with a paddle attachment, beat the butter and brown sugar until light and fluffy. Beat in the egg, egg yolk, and vanilla. With the mixer at low speed, gradually add the flour mixture into the butter mixture until combined. Remove the dough from the bowl and shape into a rectangle. Wrap in plastic wrap and refrigerate 1 hour or overnight.

Filling

2. In a medium saucepan, combine the figs and water; bring to a simmer over medium heat. Simmer until the figs are soft and tender, about 10 minutes. Transfer the figs and the cooking liquid to a food processor; add the preserves and lemon juice and zest. Process until smooth.

3. Preheat the oven to 350°F. Line 2 large baking sheets with parchment paper or use nonstick baking sheets.

4. Pour the filling into a pastry bag fitted with a ½" round tip. On a lightly floured surface, roll dough into a 24" × 6" rectangle. Pipe a 1½"-wide strip of filling down the center of the rectangle. Fold each long side of the rectangle toward the center of the strip of filling, so that the sides overlap slightly. Cut the dough crosswise into two 12" logs; refrigerate 15 minutes or overnight.

Glaze

5. In a small bowl, beat together the egg and the milk. Transfer each log, seam-side down, to a cutting board. Brush with the egg glaze, then sprinkle with the crystal sugar. Cut each log into twelve 1"-thick slices; place, 2" apart, on the prepared baking sheets. Bake 15 to 20 minutes, rotating the baking sheets between the upper and lower oven racks halfway through baking, until golden brown. Transfer the bars to wire racks to cool completely.

Makes 2 dozen bars

BROWNIES

Our brownies are fudgy, moist, and rich. Spiked with espresso powder and toasted walnuts, these are an adult version of the childhood favorite.

---

6 ounces semisweet chocolate, chopped

3 ounces bittersweet chocolate, chopped

1 cup plus 1 tablespoon granulated sugar

1 cup (2 sticks) unsalted butter

4 large eggs

1 tablespoon instant espresso powder

1 teaspoon vanilla extract

1¼ cups all-purpose flour

1 teaspoon kosher salt

1½ cups walnuts, toasted and coarsely chopped (see "Toasting Nuts," page 137)

1. Preheat the oven to 325°F. Line a 13" × 9" baking pan with foil; lightly butter the foil.

2. In a large heatproof bowl, combine the chocolates, sugar, and butter. Set the bowl over a saucepan filled with 1" of simmering water. Heat, stirring occasionally, until the chocolate and butter are melted and the mixture is smooth. Remove the bowl from the heat and set aside.

3. In another large heatproof bowl, whisk together the eggs, espresso powder, and vanilla. Set over the simmering water and stir until the eggs are just warmed and the espresso powder is dissolved. Remove the bowl from the heat.

4. In a small bowl, stir together the flour and salt. Whisk the egg mixture into the chocolate mixture; stir in the flour mixture, then the walnuts.

5. Pour the batter into the prepared pan, spreading evenly. Bake on the center oven rack for 20 to 25 minutes, or until a wooden skewer inserted into the center of the brownies comes out a little wet (this ensures the brownies will be moist and chewy). Cool the brownies in the pan completely. Cut into 15 squares.

Makes 15 squares

BLONDIES

This recipe is so packed with fruit and nuts that there is just enough batter to hold it together. The chocolate, coconut, and pecans add richness and crunch.

2¾ cups all-purpose flour

¾ teaspoon baking soda

¾ teaspoon kosher salt

1 cup (2 sticks) plus 2 tablespoons unsalted butter

2 cups firmly packed dark brown sugar

½ cup granulated sugar

2 large eggs

¾ teaspoon vanilla extract

8 ounces bittersweet chocolate chunks

1 cup pecans, toasted and coarsely chopped (see "Toasting Nuts," page 137)

1 cup unsweetened coconut chips (see note)

1 cup dried tart cherries (see Resources, page 238)

1. Preheat the oven to 325°F. Butter a 13" × 9" baking pan.

2. In a large bowl, stir together the flour, baking soda, and salt. In the bowl of a heavy-duty mixer with a paddle attachment, beat the butter and brown and granulated sugars until light and fluffy. Beat in the eggs and vanilla. At low speed, beat in the flour mixture just until combined. Fold in the chocolate chunks, pecans, coconut chips, and dried cherries.

3. Spread the batter into the prepared pan. Bake on the center oven rack 25 to 28 minutes, until light golden brown. Cool completely on a wire rack. Cut into 15 squares.

Makes 15 bars

Note:
Unsweetened coconut chips can be found in health food stores.

SMALL SWEETS

Small sweets are precious gems we make especially for our customers. Most are so small that they can be sneaked from the bag on the way home and enjoyed without anyone else ever knowing it! Whether it is biting into the thin, crackling crust of the cannele or into a moist cream-filled cupcake, they are 100 percent pleasure! Assemble your own selection of the small sweets that follow to create your own serving of "mignardises," which is French for a course of these delicacies.

CANNELE

These rustic French pastries date to medieval days when nuns made them for what we now refer to as bake sales. While they used beeswax to prevent the cakes from sticking, the little copper molds are now brushed with clarified butter or nonstick spray.

2 cups milk

2 tablespoons unsalted butter

1 vanilla bean, split lengthwise

2 large eggs

2 large egg yolks

½ cup plus 2 tablespoons all-purpose flour

¼ cup granulated sugar

Pinch of kosher salt

Grated zest of 1 orange

½ teaspoon dark rum

CLARIFYING BUTTER

Clarified butter is unsalted butter that has been melted to separate the milk solids from the liquid. It has a higher smoking point, which makes it useful for sautéing. Since it will keep for several weeks in the refrigerator, we recommend making a large quantity that is then readily available for use.

To prepare, cut 1 pound of unsalted butter into large cubes. Place in a heavy saucepot and melt over medium heat. Bring the butter just to a boil. Turn off the heat and allow the butter to cool. The milk solids will sink to the bottom of the pan. Skim foam from the surface. Slowly pour the clarified butter (the clear liquid) through a strainer lined with dampened cheesecloth into a bowl or airtight container. Do not strain the milk solids at the bottom of the pan. Refrigerate until ready to use.

1. Combine 1 cup of the milk and the butter in a small saucepan. Scrape the seeds from the vanilla bean; add the seeds and the bean to the milk mixture. Bring the mixture to a simmer over medium heat. Remove from the heat; cool to room temperature.

2. Meanwhile, whisk together the remaining 1 cup milk, eggs, and egg yolks in a large bowl. In a small bowl, combine the flour, granulated sugar, and salt. Whisk the flour mixture into the egg mixture until smooth. Stir in the cooled milk mixture. Strain the custard through a fine sieve into a medium bowl. Discard the vanilla bean. Stir in the orange zest and rum. Cover and refrigerate overnight.

3. Preheat the oven to 400°F. Spray twelve 2" × 2" copper cannele molds (see Resources, page 238) with vegetable cooking spray or brush with clarified butter (see "Clarifying Butter").

4. Stir the custard to redistribute the orange zest. Fill each prepared mold with ⅓ cup custard. Arrange the molds on a baking tray. Bake on the center oven rack 40 to 45 minutes until the tops are dark golden brown.

5. Cool the cannele in the molds 10 minutes. Unmold and cool completely on wire racks.

Makes 12 cannele

CHOCOLATE POTS DE CRÈME

These cups of smooth silky custard are satisfying alone or topped with whipped cream or Crème Fraîche (page 133). If you like, you may also sprinkle with sugar and caramelize the tops to finish them.

1 vanilla bean, split lengthwise

2¼ cups heavy cream

¾ cup milk

¼ cup plus 2 tablespoons granulated sugar

1½ tablespoons unsweetened Dutch-process cocoa

⅛ teaspoon kosher salt

9 large egg yolks

1½ tablespoons unsalted butter, softened

6 ounces bittersweet chocolate, chopped

Whipped cream and chocolate shavings, for garnish

1. Scrape out the seeds of the vanilla bean. In a large nonreactive saucepan, combine the vanilla bean and seeds, the cream, and the milk. Bring to a simmer over medium heat. Remove the pan from the heat. Cover the pan and let the cream mixture stand 5 minutes.

2. Meanwhile, in a medium bowl, stir together the sugar, cocoa, and salt. Add the egg yolks and whisk until smooth.

3. Return the cream mixture to a simmer, then whisk it into the egg yolk mixture. Scrape the custard back into the saucepan. Over medium-low heat and with a heat-proof spatula, cook the custard, stirring constantly over the bottom and sides of the pan, until the mixture is thick enough to coat the back of the spatula. Remove the pan from the heat; whisk in the butter and chocolate until smooth.

4. Pour the custard through a fine sieve into a large measuring cup. Divide the custard between eight 4- to 5-ounce custard cups. Place the custard cups on a tray. Cover each cup tightly with plastic wrap to prevent a skin from forming. Refrigerate the custards overnight until firm. Serve topped with a little whipped cream and chocolate shavings, if desired.

Makes 8 custards

Note:

Traditionally custards are baked in a water bath in order to achieve the proper consistency. Because of the quantity of chocolate and the addition of butter in this recipe, these Chocolate Pots de Crème will set and develop a rich, smooth custardy texture without being baked.

TRIPLE CHOCOLATE CUPCAKES

What could be better than a moist chocolate cake filled with rich chocolate cream and then topped with more chocolate? We are hard-pressed to think of anything. These sophisticated little cakes appeal to adults as well as children.

Cupcakes

1 recipe Chocolate Layer Cake batter
 (page 88)

Filling

¼ cup heavy cream

1 cup coarsely chopped bittersweet
 chocolate

1½ cups mascarpone cheese

Chocolate Glaze

1 cup heavy cream

1 cup coarsely chopped bittersweet
 chocolate

1 tablespoon light corn syrup

Decoration

½ cup coarsely chopped milk
 chocolate, melted

Cupcakes

1. Preheat the oven to 325°F. Spray twelve 2½" (½-cup) muffin-pan cups with nonstick spray. Prepare the cake batter as directed. Spoon the batter evenly into the prepared muffin-pan cups. Bake the cupcakes on the center oven rack 20 to 25 minutes, until a skewer inserted in the center of 1 cupcake comes out clean. Cool the cupcakes in the pan 5 minutes. Remove the cupcakes and cool completely on wire racks. Wrap well and refrigerate overnight.

Filling

2. In a small saucepan, bring the cream to a simmer over low heat. Stir in the chocolate until smooth. Remove the pan from the heat; cool the chocolate slightly. In a large bowl, soften the mascarpone with a wooden spoon until smooth. Stir in the chocolate mixture until blended. Set aside.

3. In a nonreactive saucepan, bring the cream to a simmer over medium heat. Remove from the heat. Stir in the chocolate and corn syrup until smooth. Cool the glaze, stirring occasionally.

4. With a small, sharp knife, cut a nickel-size hole in the bottom of each cupcake, but position the tip of the knife at an angle toward the center of the cupcake, so you'll remove a cone-shaped piece of cake. Reserve the cake "cones."

5. Fill a large pastry bag, fitted with a ¼" round tip, with the filling. Insert the tip in the hole of each cupcake, then pipe enough filling to fill the hole. Slice a thin disk from a reserved "cone" and seal the hole. Place each cupcake in a paper cupcake liner.

6. Spoon 1½ to 2 tablespoons chocolate glaze over the top of each cupcake; tilt each cupcake so that the top is evenly coated with the glaze.

Decoration

7. Drizzle the milk chocolate over each cupcake in a decorative pattern. Let the cupcakes stand 10 to 15 minutes or until the chocolate sets.

Makes 1 dozen

FINANCIER (SMALL ALMOND CAKES)

These moist almond treats, traditionally baked in rectangular molds, can be used in many preparations and baked in various sizes. Financiers are often served warm from the oven with a plate of confections at the end of a meal.

1 cup (2 sticks) plus 2 tablespoons butter, plus melted butter to brush the molds

1 vanilla bean

1½ cups sliced blanched almonds, lightly toasted (see "Toasting Nuts," page 137)

¾ cup + 2 tablespoons all-purpose flour

1 cup plus 6 tablespoons granulated sugar

⅛ teaspoon kosher salt

9 large egg whites

1 tablespoon honey

1 tablespoon grated lemon zest

½ teaspoon almond extract

1. In a saucepan over low heat, melt the butter with the vanilla bean. Increase the heat to medium and cook until butter becomes golden brown, 4 to 5 minutes. Immediately strain the butter through a fine sieve into a bowl. Discard the vanilla bean. Cool.

2. In a food processor, grind the almonds with the flour to a fine powder. (Do not overprocess, as the nuts will become oily.) In a bowl, stir together the almond flour, sugar, and salt. In a large bowl, whisk the egg whites lightly to break them up. Whisk in the honey, lemon zest, and almond extract. Add the almond mixture and stir to combine. Add the butter and gently mix to incorporate. Cover and refrigerate the batter 1 hour or overnight.

3. Preheat the oven to 375°F. Brush twelve 3½" × 2" barquette molds (or madeleine molds) with butter. Place the molds on a baking sheet. Pour about ¼ cup batter into each mold (2 tablespoons into each madeleine mold). Bake the cakes on the center oven rack 12 to 15 minutes (8 to 10 minutes for madeleine molds) or until the cakes are puffed and golden brown around the edges. Transfer the baking sheet to a wire rack. Cool the cakes 10 minutes, then remove the cakes from the molds. Repeat with the remaining batter. (The batter may also be covered and refrigerated up to 1 week.) Serve warm or cool completely.

Makes about 3 dozen cakes

ORANGE-TARRAGON SAVARINS

Named after the 18th-century food writer Brillat-Savarin, this rich yeast cake is normally made in a large ring and then soaked in rum syrup. Here the rum is replaced with fragrant orange and tarragon syrup, and the savarins are baked in individual brioche tins that are inverted.

½ cup (1 stick) unsalted butter, melted

1 pound, 2 ounces Brioche Dough (page 34)

2 tablespoons grated orange zest

¼ teaspoon pure orange oil (such as Boyajian; see Resources, page 238)

2 teaspoons plus ¼ cup fresh tarragon leaves, coarsely chopped

1 cup plus 2 tablespoons fresh orange juice

⅔ cup granulated sugar

½ teaspoon anise seeds

¾ cup Meyer Lemon and Lavender Marmalade (page 170) or apricot jam (optional)

Strained orange segments, berries, or Crème Fraîche (page 133) (optional)

1. Generously butter twelve ½-cup brioche à tête molds. Set aside.

2. In the bowl of a heavy-duty mixer, combine the brioche dough, orange zest, orange oil, and 2 teaspoons of the tarragon. With a dough hook attachment at low speed, gently mix the dough until all the ingredients are blended.

3. Divide the dough into 12 equal pieces. On a lightly floured surface, roll each piece into a ball. Place 1 ball, seam-side up, in each prepared mold. Place the molds on a baking sheet. Let the dough rest 5 minutes. Press the dough flat into the molds so they fill into the fluted sides. Brush the tops with melted butter. Cover the molds loosely with plastic wrap and let rise in a warm, draft-free place (such as the top of the stove), 1 hour or until the dough just comes to the tops of the molds.

4. Meanwhile, preheat the oven to 350°F. In a nonreactive saucepan, bring 1 cup of the orange juice and the sugar to a boil. Reduce the heat and simmer 5 minutes. Stir in the anise seeds and the remaining ¼ cup tarragon. Remove from heat and allow syrup to cool.

5. Uncover the molds; place a piece of parchment paper over the tops, then place 2 baking sheets on top of the parchment. Bake the savarins on the center oven rack 20 minutes. Remove the baking sheets and the parchment. Bake the savarins 5 to 10 minutes more or until golden brown. Cool the savarins on a wire rack 5 minutes.

6. Line a baking sheet with parchment. Unmold the savarins onto the prepared baking sheet. Pierce the tops of each savarin with a skewer; brush the orange syrup over the tops and sides of the savarins. Repeat brushing the savarins until all the syrup is absorbed.

7. In a small saucepan, melt the marmalade or jam with the remaining 2 tablespoons orange juice over low heat. Brush the savarins with the glaze. (This is optional.) Serve with orange segments, berries, or crème fraîche, if desired.

Makes 12 savarins

MEYER LEMON AND LAVENDER MARMALADE

1½ pounds Meyer lemons (see note)

1 standard lemon

3 cups water

4 cups granulated sugar

1 tablespoon dried lavender leaves
  (see Resources, page 238)

1. Cut stem ends from the lemons and discard. With a swivel-blade vegetable peeler, remove the yellow zest from each lemon, taking care not to remove the white pith below. Try to peel wide strips of zest; this will make your work ahead a bit easier. Be sure to scrape away any pith you accidentally remove with a small, sharp knife. Set the lemons aside.

2. Place the zest in a large nonreactive saucepan; add just enough cold water to cover. Bring the water to a boil, and boil 1 to 2 minutes. Strain the zest in a sieve and rinse under cold water. Pat dry, then cut it into thin strips. Return the strips to the same saucepan. Set aside.

3. Carefully cut the white pith from the lemons and discard. Slice the lemons into ¼"-thick rounds. Remove the seeds from the slices. Transfer the seeds to a piece of cheese-cloth and set aside.

4. Cut the lemon slices into quarters. Remove any of the thick, white center membranes, and add them to the lemon seeds. Tie the cheesecloth into a bundle with kitchen twine. Place the seed bundle in the saucepan.

5. Scrape the lemon pieces, along with any juice from the cutting board, into the saucepan. Add the 3 cups water. Cover and leave in a cool place 8 hours or overnight.

6. Uncover the saucepan; place over medium-high heat. Bring to a full boil; boil 10 minutes. Stir in the sugar. Return the mixture to a boil. Reduce the heat; gently simmer the marmalade 30 to 40 minutes, or until the temperature reaches 220°F (jelly stage) on a candy thermometer. (You may also check the jelly stage by spooning a small amount of the marmalade onto a dish. Place the dish in the freezer for 1 minute.

Remove, and run your finger through the syrup. If the separation flows back very slowly, it is ready; if not, continue cooking.) Remove the saucepan from the heat. Remove seed bundle, then stir in the lavender.

Makes 5 1/2 cups

Note:

The seeds and membranes between the citrus segments contain high amounts of natural pectin. When cooking the marmalade, it is important to simmer gently to maintain the fruit and prevent scorching. Removing the white pith and blanching the peel reduces the bitterness in the final marmalade.

BLOOD ORANGE ÉCLAIRS

This blood orange éclair is Metropolitan's rendition of the classic French éclair. After biting through the crisp pastry and the smooth chocolate glaze, the tart blood orange flavor is a total surprise.

Éclairs

1	cup milk
1	teaspoon granulated sugar
¼	teaspoon kosher salt
7	tablespoons unsalted butter, cut up
1	cup plus 2½ tablespoons all-purpose flour
4	large eggs

Blood Orange Cream

6–8	blood oranges
2	tablespoons granulated sugar
2	cups Pastry Cream (page 69)
½	cup Chocolate Glaze (page 111)

Éclairs

1. Preheat the oven to 450°F. Line 2 baking sheets with parchment paper.

2. In a medium saucepan, combine the milk, sugar, and salt. Add the butter. Bring the mixture to a boil over medium-high heat. Stir to melt the butter. Add the flour all at once. Stir vigorously with a wooden spoon until the dough leaves the sides of the pan and forms a ball. Cook, stirring, 2 minutes to dry the dough. Transfer the dough to a bowl of a heavy-duty mixer. With a paddle attachment at medium-high speed, add the eggs, one at a time, beating until thoroughly incorporated after each addition.

3. Spoon the dough into a pastry bag fitted with a ½" round tip. Pipe ten to eleven 3" × 1" éclairs per baking sheet. Bake the éclairs on the center and upper oven racks 10 minutes. Reduce the oven temperature to 400°F and bake 20 minutes more. Turn off the oven and leave the oven door ajar. Leave the éclairs in the oven about 20 minutes more, until the centers are dry.

4. Grate enough of the oranges to equal 3 tablespoons grated zest. Cut the oranges in half and juice them. Strain the juice through a sieve; measure 1¼ cups (save any remaining for another use). In a small nonreactive saucepan, combine the juice and sugar. Simmer over medium heat until the mixture is reduced to ½ cup. (The mixture will thicken slightly into a syrup.) Stir in the orange zest. Cool the syrup. In a bowl, whisk together the orange syrup and the pastry cream; refrigerate 1 hour.

5. With a serrated knife, cut off the top third of each éclair. Spoon 1 heaping tablespoon blood orange cream into the bottom of each éclair. Replace the éclair tops. Spoon 1 teaspoon of chocolate glaze over the top of each éclair. Refrigerate 15 minutes or until the glaze is set.

Makes 20 to 22 éclairs

PISTACHIO-HONEY NOUGAT

This popular European confection is soft and chewy and fragrant from honey. The green pistachios sparkle through the white nougat, while the citrus zest contrasts the sweetness.

6½ cups shelled pistachio nuts

1 vanilla bean, split lengthwise

3 extra-large egg whites

2 cups confectioners' sugar, sifted

1½ cups light honey (such as orange blossom honey)

Safflower oil

Grated zest of 1 orange

Grated zest of 1 lemon

1. Preheat the oven to 325°F. Spread the pistachios on a large baking sheet. Bake 5 minutes or until lightly toasted. Cool.

2. Scrape out the seeds of the vanilla bean. In a large heatproof bowl, whisk together the vanilla seeds, egg whites, sugar, and honey until smooth. (Save the vanilla bean for another use.)

3. Lightly brush a 17½" × 12½" baking sheet, a rubber spatula, and 1 side of a 17½" × 12½" sheet of parchment paper with oil.

4. Place the egg white mixture over a large saucepan halfway filled with simmering water. With a handheld mixer, beat the mixture at high speed about 15 minutes or until the temperature reaches 238°F (soft-ball stage) on a candy thermometer. (The mixture should whiten and hold a ribbon when the beaters are lifted.) Remove the bowl from the heat. Working quickly, with the oiled spatula, fold in the pistachios and orange and lemon zests. Scrape the nougat onto the prepared pan; spread evenly. Place the prepared parchment paper, oiled-side down, over the nougat. Then place another 17½" × 12½" baking sheet over the paper. Gently press the top baking sheet over the nougat to create an even layer.

5. Let the nougat stand in a cool, dry place 12 hours, until set. Remove top baking sheet and parchment paper, and cut into 64 squares.

Makes 64 candies

CRUNCHY MACADAMIA NUTS

Even though macadamia nuts need no further embellishment, encasing them in buttery brittle and orange-scented milk chocolate and then tossing them in a special black cocoa powder sends them through the stratosphere! If you make these for your guests, trust us—they won't last long.

1¼ cups granulated sugar

¼ cup water

4 cups raw, unsalted macadamia nuts

2 tablespoons unsalted butter

12 ounces chopped milk chocolate

¼ teaspoon Boyajian pure orange oil (see Resources, page 238) (optional)

¼ cup plus 1 tablespoon special black cocoa (see Resources, page 238)

1. In a large saucepan (preferably copper), stir together the sugar and water. Bring to a boil over medium-high heat; boil 2 to 3 minutes. Do not let the sugar color. Remove the pan from the heat. Add the nuts and stir well with a wooden spoon. The sugar will coat the nuts individually and crystallize. The crystallized sugar will be white, and the nuts will separate.

2. Return the pan to medium-high heat. Stir constantly. Gradually the sugar will melt and start to caramelize. Be sure to vigorously stir the bottom and the corners of the pan to prevent burning. When the caramel turns deep golden brown (the pan will start to smoke very quickly), immediately pour the nuts into a large bowl. Add the butter and stir vigorously. The butter will melt into the caramel and help to cool it. Continue to stir until the caramel hardens and the nuts separate. Place the bowl in the freezer at least 10 minutes, until the nuts completely cool.

3. Meanwhile, place the chocolate in a heatproof bowl. Set the bowl over a saucepan halfway filled with simmering water. Heat the chocolate until melted. Stir in the orange oil if using. Remove the bowl from the simmering water and stir the chocolate until smooth.

4. Pour the melted chocolate over the cooled nuts. Stir vigorously until the chocolate coats the nuts individually and hardens. Add the cocoa and toss the nuts to coat. Store in an airtight container in a cool, dry place up to 4 days.

Makes 4¼ cups

FLATBREADS, CRACKERS, CROSTINI, AND FOCACCIA

Our flatbreads, crackers, crostini, and focaccia are full of fresh, distinctive flavors from aromatic herbs, seeds, and wheat flour. Our matzo recipes evolved for our customers who observe the Passover tradition of not eating leavened products but missed their Metropolitan bread! Use whatever you have on hand—olives, rosemary, sun-dried tomatoes, roasted garlic—and you will wind up with lively matches for savory spreads. These recipes should be used as a guide; let the season's fresh herbs and vegetables inspire your own creations.

ROSEMARY PARMESAN BREADSTICKS

Light and crispy, these flavor-packed breadsticks are perfect to serve as a party hors d'oeuvre or as an accompaniment to a salad. Make them as long and thin as you want, for a more dramatic effect, or use the dimensions given in this recipe.

1   cup plus 2 tablespoons water (70°F)

¼   cup White Starter (page 9)

¼   cup extra-virgin olive oil, plus extra for preparation

1   package (¼ ounce) active dry yeast

2¼   cups all-purpose flour, plus extra for preparation

½   cup freshly grated Parmesan cheese

¼   cup coarsely chopped fresh rosemary

1   tablespoon roasted garlic (see "Roasting Garlic")

1   teaspoon fine sea salt

ROASTING GARLIC

Preheat oven to 350°F. Place 1 bulb of garlic on a piece of foil. Drizzle with 1 teaspoon olive oil. Wrap the garlic in the foil and place on a baking tray. Bake on the center oven rack 30 to 35 minutes or until the cloves are very soft. Unwrap the garlic and cool. Cut off the stem end of the bulb; gently squeeze the garlic from the cloves. Discard the skins.

1. In the bowl of a heavy-duty mixer, combine the water, starter, oil, and yeast. With a dough hook attachment at low speed, mix in the flour, Parmesan, rosemary, garlic, and salt until blended. Increase the speed to medium. Knead the dough 4 minutes. Transfer the dough to a lightly oiled bowl and cover tightly with plastic wrap. Let rise in a warm, draft-free place (such as the top of the stove) until doubled in size, about 2 hours.

2. Preheat the oven to 325°F. Lightly brush 3 large baking sheets with oil or use non-stick baking sheets.

3. Turn the dough out onto a lightly floured work surface. Sprinkle the dough lightly with flour and roll into a 10" × 22" rectangle. With a pastry wheel, cut the rectangle lengthwise in half to form two 5" × 22" rectangles. (Do not separate the rectangles.) Placing a pastry wheel flat against a ruler, cut across both rectangles to make two 5" × ½"-thick strips. Repeat cutting the remaining dough into strips.

4. Transfer 1 strip to a prepared baking sheet, stretching the strip slightly and twisting it twice. (It should be about 8½" long.) Press the ends of the strip onto the baking sheet to avoid shrinking and unraveling. Repeat with the remaining strips, arranging them ½" apart, to fill 1 baking sheet. Bake the breadsticks on the center oven rack 20 to 25 minutes, until light golden brown. Transfer the breadsticks to wire racks to cool completely. (Do not overbake. The breadsticks will finish crisping as they cool.) Repeat with the remaining breadsticks.

Makes 1½ pounds (about 5½ dozen)

BLACK OLIVE AND THYME MATZO

The flavor of the tart, pungent kalamata olives in this matzo is perfectly complemented by the fragrant fresh thyme.

---

2 cups all-purpose flour, plus extra for preparation

½ cup yellow cornmeal

½ cup kalamata olives, pitted and coarsely chopped

2 tablespoons fresh thyme leaves, coarsely chopped

1 teaspoon kosher salt

1½ cups cold water

1. At least 20 minutes before baking, place a large baking stone on the center oven rack. Preheat the oven to 425°F.

2. In a large bowl, stir together the flour, cornmeal, olives, thyme, and salt. Add the water and stir just until the dough comes together. Do not knead. Scrape the dough onto a flat surface; divide into 4 or 8 equal pieces. Gently shape each piece into a round.

3. Place 1 piece of the dough on a lightly floured surface; sprinkle the top with flour. With a rolling pin, roll the dough into a roughly shaped 6" or 12" circle, ⅛" thick. Flip the dough over and sprinkle with flour as needed to prevent sticking. (Do not worry about making the circle perfectly round. It will look more authentic with imperfections.)

4. Sprinkle a baker's peel or the back of a baking sheet with flour. Carefully slide the matzo onto the peel. Prick lightly with a fork. Slide the matzo onto the baking stone. Bake 3 minutes. Flip the matzo onto the other side. Bake 3 to 4 minutes more or until it is tinged golden brown and has blistered slightly. Transfer the matzo to a wire rack and cool completely. Repeat with remaining dough. The matzos will finish crisping as they cool.

Makes 4 (12") matzos or 8 (6") matzos

SUN-DRIED TOMATO MATZO

Sweet roasted garlic and flavorful sun-dried tomatoes truly elevate this crispy flatbread.

---

2 cups all-purpose flour, plus extra for preparation

½ cup sun-dried tomatoes in oil, drained and coarsely chopped

¼ cup freshly grated Parmesan cheese

1¼ teaspoons kosher salt

1 teaspoon roasted garlic (see "Roasting Garlic," page 180)

1½ cups cold water

1. At least 20 minutes before baking, place a large baking stone on the center oven rack. Preheat the oven to 425°F.

2. In a large bowl, stir together the flour, tomatoes, Parmesan, salt, and garlic. Add the water and stir just until the dough comes together. Do not knead. Scrape the dough onto a flat surface; divide into 4 or 8 equal pieces. Gently shape each piece into a round.

3. Place 1 piece of the dough on a lightly floured surface; sprinkle the top with flour. With a rolling pin, roll the dough into a roughly shaped 6" or 12" circle, ⅛" thick. Flip the dough over and sprinkle with flour as needed to prevent sticking. (Do not worry about making the circle perfectly round. It will look more authentic with imperfections.)

4. Sprinkle a baker's peel or the back of a baking sheet with flour. Carefully slide the matzo onto the peel. Prick lightly with a fork. Slide the matzo onto the baking stone. Bake 3 minutes. Flip the matzo onto the other side. Bake 3 to 4 minutes more or until it is tinged golden brown and has blistered slightly. Transfer the matzo to a wire rack and cool completely. Repeat with remaining dough. The matzos will finish crisping as they cool.

Makes 4 (12") matzos or 8 (6") matzos

Semolina Matzo

The semolina flour adds a depth and sweetness to this tasty matzo.

1½ cups semolina flour (durum)

1½ cups all-purpose flour, plus extra for preparation

2 teaspoons kosher salt

1½ cups plus 2 tablespoons cold water

1. At least 20 minutes before baking, place a large baking stone on the center oven rack. Preheat the oven to 425°F.

2. In a large bowl, stir together the semolina and all-purpose flours and salt. Add the water and stir just until the dough comes together. Do not knead. Scrape the dough onto a flat surface; divide into 6 or 12 equal pieces. Gently shape each piece into a round.

3. Place 1 piece of the dough on a lightly floured surface; sprinkle the top with flour. With a rolling pin, roll the dough into a roughly shaped 6" or 12" circle, ⅛" thick. Flip the dough over and sprinkle with flour as needed to prevent sticking. (Do not worry about making the circle perfectly round. It will look more authentic with imperfections.)

4. Sprinkle a baker's peel or the back of a baking sheet with flour. Carefully slide the matzo onto the peel. Prick lightly with a fork. Slide the matzo onto the baking stone. Bake 3 minutes. Flip the matzo onto the other side. Bake 3 to 4 minutes more or until it is tinged golden brown and has blistered slightly. Transfer the matzo to a wire rack and cool completely. Repeat with remaining dough. The matzos will finish crisping as they cool.

Makes 6 (12") matzos or 12 (6") matzos

FOCACCIA DOUGH

Focaccia is rustic bread at its best—peasant food turned gourmet in recent years. Flat bread seasoned with extra-virgin olive oil and just about anything else, focaccia sets the stage for the perfect sandwich or panini, can be used as the foundation for all kinds of appetizers, and is wonderful paired with salad or soup for a quick lunch or supper. Can you tell it's one of our favorite foods?

1 cup White Starter (page 9)

1 cup plus 1 tablespoon water (72°F)

2 teaspoons active dry yeast

2 tablespoons extra-virgin olive oil

1 tablespoon milk

3 cups bread flour, plus extra for preparation

2 teaspoons fine sea salt

1. In the bowl of a heavy-duty mixer, combine the starter, 1 cup of the water, yeast, oil, milk, and flour. With a dough hook attachment at low speed, mix 3 to 4 minutes, until the dough forms a shaggy mass. Sprinkle the salt over the dough. Let the dough rest 20 minutes.

2. At low speed, mix the salt into the dough for 1 minute. Increase the speed to medium. Add the remaining 1 tablespoon water. Knead the dough 8 minutes. Test for proper gluten development (see "Testing Gluten Development," page 17). The dough should be sticky, yet smooth. The temperature should be 78° to 80°F when tested with an instant-read thermometer.

3. Transfer the dough to a lightly oiled bowl and cover tightly with plastic wrap. Let rise in a warm, draft-free place for 1 hour. Fold the dough down to deflate. Cover the bowl and let the dough rise until doubled in size, about 1½ hours.

Makes 2 pounds dough (enough for 8 individual focaccias or 2 large focaccias)

OVEN-DRIED CHERRY TOMATO FOCACCIA

Slowly baking seasoned tomatoes concentrates their sweet flavor in this focaccia and yields a soft, pleasant texture. This recipe, and the other focaccia variations, may be prepared as two 10" focaccias. Just increase the baking time 8 to 10 minutes.

2 pints red cherry or pear-shaped tomatoes, stemmed, or 6 plum tomatoes, sliced about ¼" thick

¼ cup plus 8 teaspoons extra-virgin olive oil

1 teaspoon kosher salt

¼ teaspoon freshly ground black pepper

2 teaspoons fresh thyme leaves

½ teaspoon fresh marjoram leaves

Yellow cornmeal, for preparation

1 recipe Focaccia Dough (page 186)

4 tablespoons goat cheese

1. Preheat the oven to 275°F. In a bowl, toss together the tomatoes, ¼ cup of the oil, salt, and pepper. Spread the tomatoes in 1 layer on a baking sheet. Bake on the center oven rack to dry slowly, 12 hours. The tomatoes will look wrinkled and smaller in size, but will still be moist. Sprinkle with the thyme and marjoram and toss gently to coat.

2. Meanwhile, line 2 large baking sheets with parchment paper; sprinkle lightly with cornmeal. Divide the dough into 8 equal pieces. Shape each piece into a round. Arrange 4 pieces, at least 2½" apart, on each prepared baking sheet. Flatten each piece slightly. Cover the baking sheets loosely with plastic wrap; let the focaccia rise at room temperature 1 hour.

3. At least 20 minutes before baking, place a large baking stone on the center oven rack. Preheat the oven to 425°F.

4. Uncover the focaccia. Using your fingertips, dimple the focaccia, spreading each piece to a 6" circle and leaving a ¼" border. Divide the tomatoes or tomato slices among the focaccia. Dot each focaccia with ½ tablespoon goat cheese, tucking the cheese in between the tomatoes.

5. Very quickly, open the oven door and generously spray the entire oven cavity with water (taking care not to spray the oven lightbulb) to create steam. (See "Creating Steam in Your Oven," page 17.) Place 1 sheet of the focaccia on the baking stone. Close the oven door. Bake 1 minute. Open the oven door and spray all around the focaccia. Close the oven door. Reduce the oven temperature to 400°F. Bake the focaccia 25 to 30 minutes more, until golden. Transfer the focaccia to a wire rack; drizzle each with 1 teaspoon oil. Repeat with the remaining focaccia. Serve warm or cool completely.

Makes 8 individual focaccias

ONION FOCACCIA

Our onion focaccia is similar to the classic Provençal
pissaladiere. *You may omit the anchovies if you prefer.*

Yellow cornmeal, for preparation

1 recipe Focaccia Dough (page 186)

8 teaspoons roasted garlic (see
"Roasting Garlic," page 180)

4 anchovy fillets, cut in half
(optional)

2 cups Caramelized Onions
(page 28)

24 kalamata olives, pitted

5 tablespoons plus 1 teaspoon freshly
grated Parmesan cheese

4 teaspoons extra-virgin olive oil

1. Line 2 large baking sheets with parchment paper; sprinkle lightly with cornmeal. Divide the dough into 8 equal pieces. Shape each piece into a round. Arrange 4 pieces, at least 2½" apart, on each prepared baking sheet. Flatten each piece slightly. Cover the baking sheets loosely with plastic wrap; let the focaccia rise at room temperature 1 hour.

2. At least 20 minutes before baking, place a large baking stone on the center oven rack. Preheat the oven to 425°F.

3. Uncover the focaccia. Using your fingertips, dimple the focaccia, spreading each piece to a 6" circle and leaving a ¼" border. For each focaccia, spread 1 teaspoon roasted garlic over the center of the dough. Press ½ anchovy fillet on top, if desired. Spread ¼ cup onions over the top, leaving the border. Press 3 olives into the onions. Sprinkle each focaccia with 2 teaspoons Parmesan, then drizzle with ½ teaspoon oil.

5. Very quickly, open the oven door and generously spray the entire oven cavity with water (taking care not to spray the oven lightbulb) to create steam. (See "Creating Steam in Your Oven," page 17.) Place 1 sheet of the focaccia on the baking stone. Close the oven door. Bake 1 minute. Open the oven door and spray all around the focaccia. Close the oven door. Reduce the oven temperature to 400°F. Bake the focaccia 25 to 30 minutes more, until golden. Transfer the focaccia to a wire rack; drizzle each with 1 teaspoon oil. Repeat with the remaining focaccia. Serve warm or cool completely.

Makes 8 individual focaccias

POTATO-GOAT CHEESE FOCACCIA

Rich potato slices combined with tangy goat cheese and fruity olive oil make this focaccia very satisfying.

Yellow cornmeal, for preparation

1 recipe Focaccia Dough (page 186)

8 small red bliss potatoes (2½ pounds), sliced into ¼"-thick rounds

6 tablespoons plus 2 teaspoons extra-virgin olive oil

Salt and freshly ground black pepper, to taste

8 teaspoons roasted garlic (see "Roasting Garlic," page 180) or Basil Pesto (page 222)

5 tablespoons plus 1 teaspoon goat cheese

8 teaspoons fresh thyme, rosemary, oregano, or marjoram leaves

1. Line 2 large baking sheets with parchment paper; sprinkle lightly with cornmeal. Divide the focaccia dough into 8 equal pieces. Shape each piece into a round. Arrange 4 pieces, at least 2½" apart, on each prepared baking sheet. Flatten each piece slightly. Cover the baking sheets loosely with plastic wrap; let the focaccia rise at room temperature 1 hour.

2. Meanwhile, preheat the oven to 400°F. Spread the potatoes on a baking sheet; drizzle with 4 teaspoons of the oil, then sprinkle with salt and pepper. Roast the potatoes 12 minutes. (The potatoes will not be fully cooked; they will finish cooking as the focaccia bakes.)

3. Increase the oven temperature to 425°F. Using your fingertips, dimple the focaccia, spreading each piece to a 6" circle and leaving a ¼" border. For each focaccia, spread 1 teaspoon roasted garlic or pesto over the center of the dough. Arrange 1 circle of overlapping potato slices over the garlic, leaving the border. Dot each with 2 teaspoons goat cheese, tucking the cheese in between the potato slices. Sprinkle each with 1 teaspoon herbs, then drizzle with 1 teaspoon oil. Season with the salt and pepper.

4. Very quickly, open the oven door and generously spray the entire oven cavity with water (taking care not to spray the oven lightbulb) to create steam. (See "Creating Steam in Your Oven," page 17.) Place 1 sheet of the focaccia on the baking stone. Close the oven door. Bake 1 minute. Open the oven door and spray all around the focaccia. Close the oven door. Reduce the oven temperature to 400°F. Bake the focaccia 25 to 30 minutes more, until golden. Transfer the focaccia to a wire rack; drizzle each with 1 teaspoon oil. Repeat with the remaining focaccia. Serve warm or cool completely.

Makes 8 individual focaccias

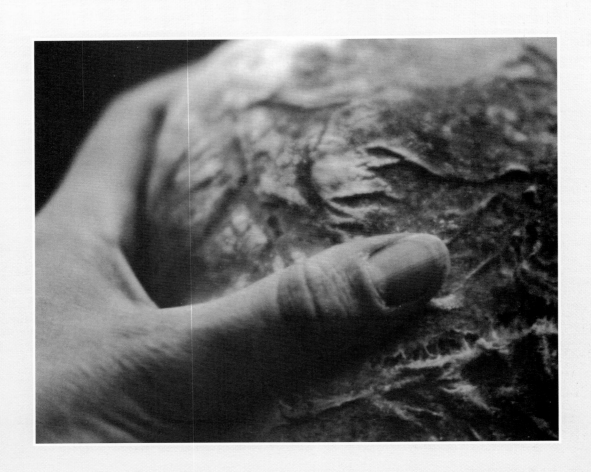

ROSEMARY FLATBREAD (CIABATTA)

A trip to Tuscany a few years ago inspired our version of flatbread. It is wonderful served warm from the oven drizzled with fragrant olive oil.

---

1 recipe Focaccia Dough (page 186)

4 tablespoons extra-virgin olive oil

2 teaspoons coarsely chopped fresh rosemary

1 teaspoon coarse sea salt

Yellow cornmeal, for preparation

1. Line 2 large baking sheets with parchment paper; sprinkle with flour. Divide the dough into 2 equal pieces. On a lightly floured surface, flatten 1 piece of dough into a roughly shaped rectangle with 1 short side facing you. Starting from a short side, roll up the length of the dough to form a cylinder. Gently roll the cylinder back and forth until it is even. (The loaf should measure about 12" × 4".) Place the loaf, seam-side down, on a prepared baking sheet; sprinkle the top with flour. Repeat with the remaining dough.

2. Cover the loaves loosely with plastic wrap. Let rise in a warm, draft-free place for 1 hour, until puffy. Meanwhile, at least 20 minutes before baking, place a large baking stone on the center oven rack. Preheat the oven to 450°F.

3. Line a baker's peel (see Resources, page 238) or the back of a baking sheet with parchment; sprinkle with cornmeal. Uncover 1 loaf; sprinkle top with flour. Carefully invert the loaf onto the prepared baker's peel; remove the top sheet of parchment paper. With fingertips, dimple the loaf until it measures 14" × 5½". Drizzle the top with 2 tablespoons oil, then sprinkle with 1 teaspoon rosemary and ½ teaspoon salt.

4. Very quickly, open the oven door and generously spray the entire oven cavity with water (taking care not to spray the oven lightbulb) to create steam. (See "Creating Steam in Your Oven," page 17.) Slide the loaf, with the parchment, onto the stone. Close the oven door. Bake 1 minute. Open the oven door and spray all around the loaf. Close the oven door. Bake 1 minute. Spray all around the loaf again. Reduce the oven temperature to 400°F. Bake the loaf 30 to 35 minutes more, until golden brown. Transfer the loaf to a wire rack. Serve warm or at room temperature. Repeat with the remaining loaf.

Makes 2 loaves

SPICED CORNMEAL CRACKERS

The earthy sweet corn flavor of these lightly spiced crackers will inspire you to replace your store-bought corn chips. They are easy to make in large quantities and then store in airtight containers for unexpected guests.

1½ cups yellow cornmeal

1½ cups all-purpose flour

1½ teaspoons kosher salt

½ teaspoon granulated sugar

½ teaspoon chili powder

½ teaspoon onion powder

½ teaspoon garlic powder

½ teaspoon ground red pepper

¼ teaspoon ground cumin

¼ teaspoon paprika

2½ cups plus 3 tablespoons cold water

1. Preheat the oven to 350°F. Line 2 large baking sheets with parchment paper.

2. In a medium bowl, whisk together the cornmeal, flour, salt, sugar, and spices. Add the water and whisk until smooth.

3. Drop ½ cup of the batter in the center of a prepared baking sheet. With an offset spatula, spread the batter into a thin sheet (1⁄16" thick). Bake the cracker on the center oven rack 15 to 20 minutes, until light golden. (The cracker will buckle up from the baking sheet.) Cool the cracker on the baking sheet on a wire rack. Repeat with the remaining batter. Serve the crackers within 1 hour of baking or store in an airtight container for up to 2 weeks.

Makes 6 crackers

SESAME-CHEDDAR CRACKERS

These flaky, crispy crackers are fun to make at home, and your friends will be impressed when you serve them alongside your favorite spreads.

---

1 teaspoon active dry yeast

1½ cups water (75°F)

¼ cup extra-virgin olive oil

2 tablespoons sour cream

3¾ cups all-purpose flour, plus extra for preparation

1¼ cups shredded sharp Cheddar cheese

½ cup sesame seeds, lightly toasted (see "Toasting Millet" instructions, page 47)

¼ cup coarsely chopped flat-leaf parsley

1¾ teaspoons kosher salt

1 large egg white, lightly beaten

1. In the bowl of a heavy-duty mixer, dissolve the yeast in the water. Add the oil, sour cream, flour, cheese, sesame seeds, parsley, and salt. With a dough hook attachment at low speed, mix the dough 1 minute. Increase the speed to medium. Knead the dough 4 minutes. Transfer the dough to a lightly oiled bowl and cover tightly with plastic wrap. Let rise in a warm, draft-free place (such as the top of the stove) until doubled in size, about 2 hours.

2. Preheat the oven to 400°F. Line 2 large baking sheets with parchment paper.

3. Divide the dough in half. Place 1 piece on a lightly floured surface; sprinkle the top with flour. With a rolling pin, roll the dough ¹⁄₁₆" thick, lifting and sprinkling the dough with more flour as needed to prevent sticking. Cut out crackers with a 1½" round cutter. With a spatula, transfer the crackers and arrange ½" apart on the prepared baking sheets. Prick each cracker generously with a fork (to prevent puffing when the crackers bake). Brush the crackers lightly with the egg white. Bake 12 to 15 minutes, until golden brown. Transfer the crackers to a wire rack to cool. Repeat with the remaining dough. Store the crackers in an airtight container.

Makes about 5½ dozen

CHARCOAL-GRILLED TOMATO AND GOAT CHEESE CROSTINI

At a celebration dinner at the home of our friend Kevin von Klause, we were presented with these beautiful summer crostini. We loved them so much we asked him if we could include his recipe, which he generously contributes here.

8 ounces creamy fresh goat cheese, at room temperature

1 bunch basil, washed and dried (see "Washing Leafy Greens," page 207)

1 Country Bread (page 14) or Rosemary Flatbread (Ciabatta) (page 195), cut crosswise into 8 (½"-thick) slices

1 clove garlic, peeled

¼ cup extra-virgin olive oil

2 large, ripe, juicy tomatoes (about 1½ pounds), sliced ½" thick

½ teaspoon kosher salt

½ teaspoon freshly ground black pepper

1. Preheat the grill.

2. In a bowl, mix the goat cheese with a fork until it is smooth and easily spreadable. Pick the basil leaves from the stems and set aside, covered with a damp cloth.

3. Rub 1 side of the bread slices with the garlic clove, then brush both sides with some of the oil. Place the bread slices, garlic-side down, on the grill. Grill over medium heat until toasted, about 2 minutes.

4. Meanwhile, place the tomato slices on a large plate; sprinkle with the salt and pepper and drizzle with the remaining oil. Grill the tomatoes about 2 minutes per side.

5. Remove the bread from the grill and spread the toasted side with the goat cheese. Return the bread to the grill, cheese side up, and grill 2 minutes.

6. Transfer the crostini to a cutting board. Top with the basil leaves and the grilled tomatoes. Cut each crostini in half and serve.

Makes 16 crostini

FAVA BEAN CROSTINI

Although shelling, blanching, and peeling fresh fava beans is a tedious process, the outcome is well worth the trouble. The fresh mint is a critical ingredient because it brightens the flavor of this rich crostini.

Fava Bean Puree

2½ pounds fresh fava beans

¼ cup plus 1 tablespoon extra-virgin olive oil

½ teaspoon minced garlic

½ teaspoon kosher salt

¼ teaspoon freshly ground black pepper

1 teaspoon coarsely chopped fresh mint

1 teaspoon coarsely chopped flat-leaf parsley

Bread

6 (½"-thick) slices Country Bread (page 14)

2 tablespoons extra-virgin olive oil

2 cloves garlic, cut in half

Fresh mint or parsley leaves, for garnish

Fava Bean Puree

1. Open the fava pods and remove the beans. In a saucepan, bring 2 cups of water to a boil. Add the beans and boil 1 minute. Drain the beans and cool under cold running water. Pierce the smooth top of the shells with your thumbnail and squeeze out the beans inside. You should have about 1¾ cups of beans.

2. In a large sauté pan, heat 1 tablespoon of the oil over medium–low heat. Add the garlic and beans. Cook the beans, stirring, 1 minute. Add the salt, pepper, and ¼ cup water. Cook 6 to 8 minutes, until the beans become tender and liquid evaporates. Remove the pan from the heat. Transfer the beans to a food processor; add the remaining ¼ cup oil, mint, and parsley. Puree until smooth.

3. Preheat the oven to 375°F, or preheat a broiler or grill. Arrange the bread on a baking sheet; brush the tops with the oil. Bake, broil, or grill about 3 to 4 minutes per side, until toasted. Rub each slice with the cut side of a garlic clove; spread each with a generous 2 tablespoons of the fava bean puree. Garnish with the mint or parsley leaves.

Makes 6 crostini

EGG AND BROCCOLI RABE BRUSCHETTA

This bruschetta is fun to serve as a first course to a meal or Sunday breakfast or on its own. It was inspired by the enotecas of Italy, where crostini and bruschetta are the focus and local ingredients highlight the menu.

6 (½"-thick) slices Country Bread (page 14) or Potato-Rosemary Bread (page 18)

6 tablespoons extra-virgin olive oil

2 cloves garlic, cut in half

2 bunches broccoli rabe, thick stems removed

½ teaspoon minced garlic

1 teaspoon kosher salt

½ teaspoon freshly ground black pepper

½ teaspoon fresh lemon juice

2 teaspoons unsalted butter

6 large eggs (preferably organic brown eggs)

2–3 teaspoons white truffle oil

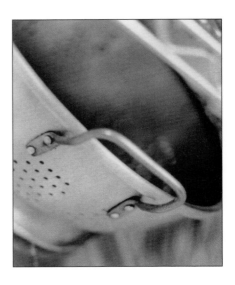

1. Preheat the oven to 375°F, or preheat a broiler or grill. Arrange the bread on a baking sheet; brush the tops with 2 tablespoons of the oil. Bake, broil, or grill about 3 to 4 minutes per side, until toasted. Rub each slice with the cut side of a garlic clove. Set aside.

2. Bring a 2-quart pot of water to a boil. Add a large pinch of salt. Put the broccoli rabe into the water and boil 1 minute. Quickly drain it and plunge it into a large bowl filled with ice water. Remove the broccoli rabe and dry; chop coarsely.

3. Heat a large sauté pan over medium-high heat. Add 2 tablespoons of the oil and the garlic. Cook briefly so garlic does not color. Stir in the broccoli rabe, ½ teaspoon salt, and ¼ teaspoon pepper. Cook 4 to 5 minutes, until broccoli rabe is tender. Stir in the lemon juice. Divide the broccoli rabe among the prepared toasts.

4. Heat 2 sauté pans over medium heat. Add 1 tablespoon olive oil and 1 teaspoon butter to each pan. Carefully crack 3 eggs into each pan, leaving space between. Season the eggs with the remaining ½ teaspoon salt and ¼ teaspoon pepper. Cover the pans and cook the eggs 4 to 5 minutes. (If you prefer hard-cooked eggs, cook 8 to 10 minutes.) With a spatula, lift 1 egg at a time and place on a bruschetta. Drizzle each bruschetta with white truffle oil. Serve immediately or warm.

Makes 6 bruschetta

SANDWICHES

Sandwiches can be simple or complex, provide a quick lunch, or be incorporated into a satisfying dinner. With the influx of panini cafés, sandwiches have become a central menu focus instead of an afterthought. Whether they are created from leftovers in your fridge or designed around specific ingredients just purchased from your farmers' market, always leave room for adding your own special twist . . . just be certain to start with the perfect loaf of bread!

PROSCIUTTO AND ASIAGO SANDWICH

This is a grown-up version of the ham and cheese sandwich, using exquisite ingredients.

4   pieces (6") French Baguette
    (page 32), split

8   teaspoons extra-virgin olive oil

8   slices (⅛"-thick each) Asiago cheese

8   thin slices of prosciutto di Parma

Freshly ground black pepper

1. Heat a sandwich press to medium–high. Tear out a little bread from the center of each baguette half and discard. Drizzle the inside of each half with 1 teaspoon oil; place 1 slice Asiago on each. Arrange 2 slices prosciutto on each bottom half of baguette; sprinkle with pepper.

2. Close each sandwich. Press down firmly on the sandwiches with your palm to compact the ingredients. Place each sandwich in the sandwich press and heat 4 to 5 minutes, or until toasted and the cheese is melted.

Tip: Alternatively, heat a large skillet over medium heat. Add the sandwiches; cover with a heavy lid, small enough so that the lid rests directly on the sandwiches, and cook 2 to 2½ minutes. Turn the sandwiches. Cover and cook 2 to 2½ minutes more, until toasted and the cheese is melted.

Makes 4 sandwiches

METROPOLITAN BLT

This recipe shows how wonderful ingredients can elevate the mundane to the exceptional.

12 slices Country Bread (page 14) or any sturdy sandwich bread, toasted

12 heaping tablespoons Roasted Garlic–Lemon Aioli (page 224)

1 bunch arugula leaves, washed, dried, and stems trimmed (see "Washing Leafy Greens")

16 slices applewood smoked bacon, cooked until crisp

3 vine-ripened tomatoes, sliced ¼" thick

1. Spread each slice of the toasted bread with 1 heaping tablespoon aioli.

2. For each sandwich, arrange an overlapping layer of arugula leaves on 1 slice of bread. Break 2 slices of the bacon in half and place on top of the arugula. Place 2 slices tomato on top of the bacon. Top with another slice of bread, then repeat with the arugula, 2 slices bacon, and 2 slices tomato. Place a third slice of bread, aioli-side down, on top. Press down firmly on each sandwich. Cut each sandwich into 2 triangles.

Makes 4 sandwiches

WASHING LEAFY GREENS

To wash leafy greens, fill a large bowl with cold water. Plunge the greens into the water and swish around. Let them rest for up to 2 minutes, so that the greens float to the top and sand or grit sinks to the bottom. Carefully scoop the greens from the water without disturbing the sand or grit in the bowl. Place the greens into a salad spinner and spin dry. Sometimes greens (particularly those with roots intact such as arugula and basil) need to be washed twice. Spread on a tea towel to dry. Store in a plastic bag or in a bowl with a moist kitchen towel over the top.

GRILLED GRUYÈRE CHEESE AND APPLE-CURRANT CHUTNEY

This sandwich was inspired by a delicious lunch we had in a pub in London—a terrific combination of country bread, sharp cheese, and pungent chutney.

8 slices Country Bread (page 14) or traditional peasant-style bread

16 (⅛"-thick) slices Gruyère cheese

8 heaping tablespoons Apple-Currant Chutney

1. Heat a sandwich press to medium–high.

2. Arrange 2 slices Gruyère on each slice of bread. Spread 2 heaping tablespoons chutney on 4 slices of the bread. Close each sandwich. Place each sandwich in the sandwich press and heat 4 to 5 minutes, or until toasted and the cheese is melted.

Tip: Alternatively, in a large skillet, melt 1 tablespoon butter over medium heat. Add 2 sandwiches. Cover the sandwiches with a heavy lid, small enough so the lid rests directly on the sandwiches, and cook 2 to 3 minutes, until lightly toasted. Turn the sandwiches; add another tablespoon butter to the skillet. Cover and cook 2 to 3 minutes more, until toasted and the cheese is melted. Repeat process with 2 more tablespoons butter and the remaining sandwiches.

Makes 4 sandwiches

APPLE-CURRANT CHUTNEY

¾ pound onions, chopped

¾ cup firmly packed dark brown sugar

½ cup granulated sugar

1 clove garlic, minced

1 tablespoon canola oil

1 cup water

5 medium Granny Smith apples, peeled and cored

Grated zest of 2 lemons

¼ cup balsamic vinegar

1 tablespoon grated fresh ginger

2 teaspoons kosher salt

⅛ teaspoon ground cinnamon

⅛ teaspoon ground cloves

⅛ teaspoon ground nutmeg

1½ cups dried currants

Juice of 2 lemons

1. In a heavy saucepot, combine the onions, brown sugar, granulated sugar, garlic, oil, and water. Bring to a boil. Reduce the heat to medium-low and cook, stirring frequently to prevent scorching, until the onions are tender and the mixture becomes very thick and syrupy, 10 to 15 minutes.

2. Dice 2 of the apples. Stir the apples into the onion mixture with the lemon zest, vinegar, ginger, salt, cinnamon, cloves, and nutmeg. Cook until the apples soften and the mixture thickens, 5 to 8 minutes.

3. Dice the remaining 3 apples. Stir the apples into the onion mixture with the currants and the lemon juice. Cook, stirring frequently, until the apples are just tender and the chutney thickens, 10 to 15 minutes. Cool the chutney to room temperature; transfer to a covered container, and refrigerate up to 2 weeks.

Makes 2 cups

Fresh Mozzarella, Basil, and Tomato Jam Sandwich

This sandwich is best made when summer tomatoes are at their peak flavor in August and September. Here we've replaced the fresh tomatoes with our own Tomato Jam so it can be made successfully in the dead of winter. This sandwich can be served as is or toasted in a sandwich press.

---

4 rustic rolls (such as *ciabatta*), split

8 tablespoons Tomato Jam

28 fresh basil leaves, washed and dried (see "Washing Leafy Greens," page 207)

16 (¼"-thick) slices fresh mozzarella

1. Tear out a little bread from the center of each roll half and discard. Spread each half with 1 tablespoon Tomato Jam.

2. For each sandwich, top the bottom half of a roll with 4 basil leaves. Arrange 4 slices mozzarella on top of the basil, then add 3 basil leaves on top of the mozzarella. Add the top half of the roll.

Makes 4 sandwiches

TOMATO JAM

2   pounds plum tomatoes, diced

1   tablespoon granulated sugar

¼   teaspoon kosher salt

¼   teaspoon balsamic vinegar

Combine all the ingredients in a nonreactive saucepan. Cook, stirring, over medium heat until the tomatoes release their juices and the mixture comes to a boil. Reduce the heat and simmer, stirring occasionally, until most of the liquid evaporates and the mixture thickens, 18 to 20 minutes. Cool the jam to room temperature; transfer to a covered container, and refrigerate up to 2 weeks.

Makes 1 ¼ cups

TUNA, EGG, AND WATERCRESS SANDWICH

In the south of France, there is a delicious sandwich called pan bagnat. *Our version has the addition of fresh mint and basil, which offers a perfect contrast to the richness of the tuna.*

---

1 (¾-pound) ahi tuna steak, ¾" thick

1 tablespoon olive oil

   Salt and freshly ground black pepper, to taste

¼ pound *haricots vert* (French green beans), blanched, cooled, and cut into ½" pieces

¼ red onion, minced

4 fresh basil leaves, washed, dried, and torn

4 large fresh mint leaves, washed, dried, and torn

½ cup Herb Vinaigrette

4 Metropolitan's Brioche Sandwich Buns (page 35) or other sandwich buns, split

1 bunch watercress, washed, dried, and stems trimmed (see "Washing Leafy Greens," page 207)

2 large hard-cooked eggs (see note)

1. Brush both sides of the tuna with the oil. Rub with salt and pepper. Place a sauté pan over high heat until it begins to smoke. Add the tuna and sear for 2 minutes. Turn the tuna and sear for another 2 minutes. Transfer the tuna to a cutting board and cool.

2. Cut the tuna into large chunks and place in a large bowl. Add the *haricots vert*, red onion, basil, mint, and ¼ cup of the vinaigrette.

3. Divide the tuna mixture among the bottom halves of the brioche. In a large bowl, toss the watercress with the remaining ¼ cup of the vinaigrette. Divide the watercress among the sandwiches. Cut each hard-cooked egg into 6 slices, discarding the ends without the yolk. Place 3 egg slices over the top of each sandwich. Add the top halves of the brioche.

Makes 4 sandwiches

Note:

To hard-cook an egg perfectly (and prevent the green discoloration that occurs around the yolk), place the egg in a saucepan, add enough cold water just to cover the egg. Bring the water to a boil over high heat. Turn off the heat; cool the egg and the water to room temperature. Peel.

HERB VINAIGRETTE

3   tablespoons fresh lemon juice

2   tablespoons balsamic vinegar

6   fresh basil leaves, washed and dried

4   fresh mint leaves, washed and dried

3   anchovy fillets

2   teaspoons Dijon mustard

1   clove garlic, minced

½   shallot

¼   teaspoon salt

¼   teaspoon freshly ground black pepper

1   cup extra-virgin olive oil

In a blender or food processor, process the lemon juice, vinegar, basil, mint, anchovy, mustard, garlic, shallot, salt, and pepper until blended, about 1 minute. With the machine running, gradually add the oil in a thin, steady stream through the feed tube, and process until the vinaigrette is smooth and emulsified.

Makes 1 ½ cups

SEARED CHICKEN AND MAYTAG BLUE CHEESE SANDWICH

Our customers love Maytag blue cheese, a top seller in our stores, because of its rich, subtle sharpness. In this sandwich, it is a wonderful complement to the sweet, spicy chicken.

¼ cup honey

1 jalapeño chile pepper, minced

1 tablespoon grated fresh ginger

1 clove garlic, minced

½ teaspoon ground cumin

½ cup soy sauce

Juice of 1 orange

Juice of 1 lemon

Juice of 1 lime

¼ cup extra-virgin olive oil

4 boneless, skinless chicken breasts

1 tablespoon olive oil

8 tablespoons Maytag Blue Cheese Dressing

4 rustic sandwich rolls, split

1 large avocado, cut into 12 slices

4 (⅛"-thick) slices red onion

1 head Bibb lettuce, washed, dried, and leaves separated (see "Washing Leafy Greens," page 207)

1. In a small bowl, combine the honey, jalapeño, ginger, garlic, and cumin; whisk in the soy sauce and citrus juices. Whisk in the extra-virgin olive oil. Add the chicken; toss to coat with the marinade. Cover and marinate the chicken in the refrigerator for up to 4 hours.

2. Preheat the oven to 350°F. Heat a large sauté pan over high heat until it is smoking.

3. Meanwhile, remove the chicken from the marinade; gently blot with paper towels (do not wipe dry). Add the olive oil to the pan. Carefully place the chicken breasts, smooth-side down, in the hot pan; cook about 3 minutes or until caramelized. Turn the chicken over and cook 2 more minutes. Transfer the chicken to a baking dish; bake 5 to 8 minutes or until cooked through. Cool slightly.

4. Spread 1 tablespoon Maytag Blue Cheese Dressing on the bottom half of each roll. Cut each chicken breast into strips and arrange 1 breast on each bottom half. Top each chicken breast with 3 slices avocado, 1 slice red onion, and 1 tablespoon dressing. Divide the lettuce among the sandwiches; add top halves of the rolls.

Makes 4 sandwiches

MAYTAG BLUE CHEESE DRESSING

1 large egg

1 teaspoon freshly ground black pepper

1 clove garlic

1 teaspoon Dijon mustard

1 teaspoon fresh lemon juice

1 cup safflower or canola oil

½ cup sour cream

4 ounces Maytag blue cheese (or any rich, creamy blue cheese)

⅛ teaspoon ground red pepper

In a food processor or blender, process the egg, black pepper, garlic, mustard, and lemon juice until blended, about 1 minute. With the machine running, gradually add the oil in a thin, steady stream through the feed tube, and process until the mixture is smooth and emulsified. Add the sour cream and process until smooth. Add the blue cheese and red pepper; pulse just until the dressing is smooth and very small pieces of the blue cheese are evenly distributed.

Makes 2 cups

PORTOBELLO, SWISS CHARD, AND GOAT CHEESE WITH WALNUT PESTO

This sandwich is filled with wonderful textures and flavors. The walnut pesto offers a quiet, underlying flavor to the sharpness of the goat cheese and the sweetness of the bell peppers. The portobello mushroom anchors the sandwich beautifully.

Mushrooms

- 2 large portobello mushrooms, stems removed
- 1 tablespoon extra-virgin olive oil
- 2 teaspoons balsamic vinegar
- 1 teaspoon soy sauce
- ½ teaspoon kosher salt
- ½ teaspoon freshly ground black pepper

Swiss Chard

- 1 tablespoon olive oil
- 1 clove garlic, minced
- 1 bunch Swiss chard, washed, dried, and thick stems removed (see "Washing Leafy Greens," page 207)

- ⅛ teaspoon kosher salt
- ⅛ teaspoon freshly ground black pepper
- 2 tablespoons water
- 1 tablespoon fresh lemon juice
- 4 (6") pieces French Baguette (page 32)
- 8 tablespoons Walnut and Sage Pesto (page 223)
- 1 large roasted red bell pepper, cut into 8 strips (see "Roasting Peppers")
- 4 ounces goat cheese, crumbled

Mushrooms

1. Preheat the oven to 375°F. In a bowl, combine the mushrooms with the extra-virgin oil, vinegar, soy sauce, salt, and pepper. Transfer the mushrooms to a baking tray. Roast 15 to 18 minutes, until cooked through. Set aside and cool.

Swiss Chard

2. In a large sauté pan, heat the oil over medium heat. Add the garlic and cook just until fragrant, 1 minute (do not color the garlic). Stir in the Swiss chard; sprinkle with the salt and ground pepper. Add the water and lemon juice. Cook until the chard is wilted, 3 to 5 minutes. Transfer the chard to a colander; drain and cool.

3. Cut each mushroom into 4 slices. Cut each baguette lengthwise in half with a serrated knife, but do not cut all the way through. Open each baguette slightly, and spread each bottom half with 2 tablespoons pesto. Divide the chard among the baguettes. Top each sandwich with 2 mushroom slices, 2 red pepper strips, and one-quarter of the goat cheese. Close the sandwiches.

Makes 4 sandwiches

ROASTING PEPPERS

Using a pair of tongs, place a bell pepper over a high flame of a gas burner. Rotate the pepper as each side chars. When the entire pepper is charred, transfer to a sturdy brown paper bag and close. Let the pepper steam and cool in the bag. (At this point the pepper may be refrigerated overnight.) Remove the pepper from the bag and peel away the charred skin. Do not rinse. Carefully make a slit from the stem end to the bottom of the pepper; open the pepper so it lies flat on a cutting board. Remove the stem and the seeds; cut and discard the white ribs, which make the pepper bitter. If roasting a quantity of peppers, arrange the peppers in a jar; add 1 peeled garlic clove and a sprig of fresh herbs (such as thyme, rosemary, or oregano). Add enough extra-virgin olive oil to cover the peppers. Cover the jar and refrigerate the peppers for up to 3 weeks.

FALAFEL SANDWICH

Traditionally, falafel is made with dried chickpeas that have been soaked overnight, drained, and then ground. We prefer the texture of the more easily digestible precooked chickpeas.

2 teaspoons ground cumin

¼ teaspoon paprika

2 cups canned chickpeas, rinsed and drained

½ cup white onion, coarsely chopped

⅓ cup fresh flat-leaf parsley leaves, washed and dried (see "Washing Leafy Greens," page 207)

⅓ cup fresh cilantro leaves, washed and dried

2 cloves garlic, minced

2 tablespoons all-purpose flour

1 tablespoon yellow cornmeal

1 teaspoon kosher salt

Canola oil, for frying

4 (8") round focaccia or pita breads

8 leaves romaine or iceberg lettuce

8 heaping tablespoons Cucumber Salad

4 teaspoons Tahini Sauce

1. In a small sauté pan, toast the cumin and paprika over low heat until fragrant, about 1 minute. Combine the spices, chickpeas, onion, parsley, cilantro, garlic, flour, cornmeal, and salt in a food processor. Pulse just until the ingredients are combined and the chickpeas are coarsely chopped (do not overprocess; this mixture should not be a smooth paste). Divide the falafel mixture into 4 equal portions. Form into balls with floured hands. Place on a baking tray and flatten each ball into a ½"-thick patty. Cover and refrigerate 1 hour or overnight, until firm.

2. In a large sauté pan, heat the oil over medium heat. (To check if the oil is hot enough, sprinkle a pinch of cornmeal into the oil. The oil will bubble if it is ready.) Add the falafel patties and brown 2 minutes on each side. Transfer to paper towels to drain.

3. Slice 1 end off each of the breads; open each to create a pocket. Fill each pocket with 2 lettuce leaves and a falafel. Carefully add 2 heaping tablespoons Cucumber Salad to each sandwich, then drizzle each with 1 teaspoon Tahini Sauce.

Makes 4 sandwiches

CUCUMBER SALAD

2 teaspoons ground cumin

2 pickling cucumbers

¼ cup plain yogurt

¼ cup sour cream

¼ cup fresh cilantro leaves, washed
   and dried

1 tablespoon fresh lemon juice

1 teaspoon extra-virgin olive oil

1 teaspoon minced garlic

1 teaspoon cracked black pepper

½ teaspoon kosher salt

1. In a small sauté pan, toast the cumin over low heat until fragrant, about 1 minute.

2. Peel the cucumbers. Cut each in half lengthwise; remove the seeds. Slice each half crosswise into ¼"-thick slices.

3. Place the cucumbers in a large bowl. In a small bowl, whisk together the cumin and the remaining ingredients. Pour over the cucumbers; stir well to combine.

Makes 1 ⅓ cups

TAHINI SAUCE

¼ cup tahini

¼ cup hot water

1 tablespoon fresh lemon juice

¼ teaspoon granulated sugar

¼ teaspoon kosher salt

In a small bowl, whisk together all ingredients until smooth.

Makes ½ cup

SPREADS AND SALADS

It didn't take long for us to see that our customers wanted "go-withs" for our breads. Early in our history, we created a range of sandwiches and spreads for our stores to carry for lunches and snacks. We continue to add to this popular line, offering boldly flavored recipes that help people throw a meal together at a moment's notice. The emphasis is on intense flavors, simple and fresh ingredients, and a mix of bright colors and textures that stand alone with bread or work well with pasta, grilled chicken, or fish. Working with a closely knit group of local purveyors—including Branch Creek Farm, Shelburne Farms, Vermont Butter and Cheese Company, and Greystone Nubians—we now offer these go-withs at most of our retail stores.

BASIL PESTO

The Italian word pesto *means "a mix of ingredients." Basil pesto is the most familiar of pestos, and it's the perfect way to use this abundant herb from your summer garden.*

---

5 garlic cloves

4 cups (2 large bunches) packed fresh basil leaves, washed and dried (see "Washing Leafy Greens," page 207)

½ cup toasted pine nuts (see "Toasting Nuts," page 137)

1 cup extra-virgin olive oil

½ cup freshly grated Parmesan cheese

1 teaspoon orange juice

¼ teaspoon salt

⅛ teaspoon freshly ground black pepper

In a food processor, process the garlic until coarsely chopped. Add the basil and pine nuts; pulse until chopped. With the machine running, gradually add the oil in a thin, steady stream through the feed tube, and process until the mixture is blended. Add the Parmesan, orange juice, salt, and pepper; process until smooth.

Tip: Adding orange juice helps slow down oxidation, which causes the pesto to discolor.

Makes 2¼ cups

Walnut and Sage Pesto

We use this luxurious sauce on our roasted eggplant sandwich. Serve it as an accompaniment to a cheese course instead of using chutney or preserves.

¾ cup extra-virgin olive oil

6 fresh sage leaves

1 shallot

1 clove garlic

2 cups toasted walnuts (see "Toasting Nuts," page 137)

¼ teaspoon salt

¼ teaspoon freshly ground pepper

1. In a small sauté pan, heat 2 tablespoons of the oil over medium heat until warm. Add the sage leaves and sauté 1 minute until fragrant. Remove the pan from the heat and cool.

2. In a food processor, pulse the shallot and garlic until minced. Add the walnuts, sage and oil mixture, salt, and pepper; pulse until the nuts are chopped. With the machine running, gradually add the remaining oil in a thin, steady stream through the feed tube, and process just until blended.

Makes 1½ cups

ROASTED GARLIC–LEMON AIOLI

This sweet and garlicky mayonnaise has great versatility and impact. It is wonderful used in sandwiches or brushed on crostini, as an accompaniment to bouillabaisse or simply served along with your favorite fish.

1　large egg, at room temperature (see note)

1　large egg yolk, at room temperature

3　tablespoons fresh lemon juice

1　clove roasted garlic (see "Roasting Garlic," page 180)

1　teaspoon Dijon mustard

　　Salt and freshly ground black pepper, to taste

2　cups extra-virgin olive oil

　　Grated zest of 1 lemon

In a food processor, process the egg, egg yolk, lemon juice, roasted garlic, mustard, salt, and pepper until blended. With the machine running, slowly add the oil in a thin, steady stream through the feed tube, and process until it is incorporated and the mixture is emulsified. Add the lemon zest and process a few seconds longer until blended.

Makes 2 cups

Note:

In order for the eggs to incorporate all the olive oil, they should be at room temperature. (If they are cold, emulsification will not occur.) To warm the eggs quickly, place them in a small bowl and add enough warm water to cover. Let stand 2 to 3 minutes. Remove the eggs from the water and proceed with the recipe as directed.

TUSCAN WHITE BEAN SPREAD

This healthy alternative to butter is most satisfying served warm on grilled or toasted bread and drizzled with a fruity, extra-virgin olive oil.

½ pound (1¼ cups) dried cannellini beans, picked over and rinsed

6 cups cold water

2 bay leaves

1 cup extra-virgin olive oil

½ cup roasted garlic (from about 3 heads) (see "Roasting Garlic," page 180)

1 teaspoon Dijon mustard

1 teaspoon fresh thyme

1 teaspoon kosher salt

1 teaspoon fresh lemon juice

½ teaspoon freshly ground black pepper

¼ teaspoon ground red pepper

1. Combine the beans and the water in a large pot. Cover and let the beans soak overnight.

2. Add the bay leaves to the soaked beans. Cover the pot and bring to a boil. Reduce the heat and simmer until the beans are very soft, about 45 minutes.

3. Drain the beans, reserving ¼ cup of the cooking liquid. Transfer the beans and the reserved cooking liquid to a food processor. Add the remaining ingredients; process until smooth. Serve warm or cool as a spread for sandwiches.

Makes 2 cups

BABA GHANOUSH

Baba ghanoush was one of the first spreads we made at Metropolitan. It has remained a staple in our kitchen and is used on roasted chicken sandwiches and with our flatbreads. Slowly roasting the eggplant helps sweeten the flesh and reduce the bitterness.

2 large eggplants

1 jalapeño chile pepper

1 teaspoon ground cumin

2 tablespoons tahini

2 tablespoons fresh lemon juice

1 tablespoon roasted garlic (see "Roasting Garlic," page 180)

1 tablespoon extra-virgin olive oil

1 teaspoon kosher salt

½ teaspoon freshly ground black pepper

⅛ teaspoon ground red pepper

1. Preheat the oven to 400°F. Lightly prick the eggplants all over with a fork. Place the eggplants and jalapeño on a baking tray. Bake until they collapse and the eggplants release their juices, 30 to 35 minutes.

2. When cool enough to handle, remove the stems and cut each eggplant lengthwise in half. Remove the seeds and scrape out the flesh; discard the skins. Remove the stem from the jalapeño, cut in half lengthwise and remove seeds.

3. In a small sauté pan, toast the cumin over low heat until fragrant, about 1 minute.

4. Transfer the eggplant and jalapeño to a food processor. Add the cumin, tahini, lemon juice, roasted garlic, oil, salt, black pepper, and red pepper; process until smooth.

Makes 1¾ cups

BLACK OLIVE TAPENADE

Both black and green olives are from the same tree. Green olives are picked in the summer while premature, and they are a wonderful substitute for the black olives used in this recipe. Tapenade is delicious mixed with pasta, used alongside fish, or simply spread on your favorite bread.

3 cups kalamata olives, pitted

½ cup extra-virgin olive oil

Juice and grated zest of 1 lemon

3 cloves garlic

2 tablespoons coarsely chopped flat-leaf parsley

1 anchovy fillet

½ teaspoon freshly ground black pepper

Rinse the olives under cold water to remove excess brine. In a food processor, pulse the olives and the remaining ingredients just until the olives are coarsely chopped and ingredients are blended. (If you prefer a smoother texture, process the mixture until smooth.)

Makes 2¼ cups

ROMESCO SAUCE

*Ground toasted nuts and bread crumbs add body and richness,
and the caramelized juices from the charred tomatoes lend a
robust sweetness to this spicy sauce from Spain.*

3 plum tomatoes

1 jalapeño chile pepper

1 large roasted red bell pepper (see
"Roasting Peppers," page 217)

¾ cup whole blanched almonds,
toasted and finely ground (see
"Toasting Nuts," page 137)

¾ cup dried bread crumbs (preferably
homemade)

¼ cup roasted garlic (1 to 2 heads)
(see "Roasting Garlic," page 180)

2 tablespoons sherry vinegar

1 teaspoon kosher salt

½ teaspoon freshly ground black
pepper

1 cup extra-virgin olive oil

1. Preheat the oven to 450°F. Place tomatoes and jalapeño in a small baking dish. Roast
until the tomatoes and jalapeño are charred and their juices have been released, 20 to
25 minutes. When cool enough to handle, peel the tomatoes and jalapeño; remove the
seeds.

2. In a food processor, process the tomatoes, jalapeño, any juices from the baking dish,
the roasted pepper, almonds, bread crumbs, roasted garlic, vinegar, salt, and pepper until
blended. With the machine running, gradually add the oil in a thin, steady stream until
incorporated and smooth.

Makes 2¼ cups

ARTICHOKE SALSA

This recipe uses prepared artichokes for ease of preparation. However, fresh baby artichokes may be substituted for those who are more adventurous.

½ cup packed fresh basil leaves, washed and dried (see "Washing Leafy Greens," page 207)

3 cloves garlic

1 (6-ounce) jar artichokes in olive oil, drained

1 large roasted red bell pepper (see "Roasting Peppers," page 217)

½ cup kalamata olives, pitted

½ cup Atalanti green olives, pitted

½ cup freshly grated Parmesan cheese

½ cup toasted walnuts (see "Toasting Nuts," page 137)

Juice and grated zest of 1 lemon

1 teaspoon freshly ground black pepper

½ teaspoon kosher salt

¾ cup extra-virgin olive oil

In a food processor, process the basil and garlic until the garlic is minced. Add the artichokes, roasted pepper, olives, Parmesan, and walnuts; pulse 2 or 3 times, just until the ingredients are combined. Add the lemon juice, lemon zest, black pepper, salt, and oil; pulse just until the ingredients are coarsely chopped.

Makes 3 cups

EVERYDAY VINAIGRETTE

A simple vinaigrette is usually 3 parts oil to 1 part vinegar. In ours, we love the way the Dijon mustard adds a light, creamy texture, while the lemon juice makes it bright and fresh but not overbearing for even the most delicate of lettuces.

½ cup loosely packed fresh basil leaves, washed and dried (optional) (see "Washing Leafy Greens," page 207)

1 cup fresh lemon juice

¼ cup Dijon mustard

¼ cup minced red onion

2 cloves garlic

½ tablespoon kosher salt

¾ teaspoon freshly ground black pepper

½ teaspoon granulated sugar

1¼ cups grapeseed oil

¾ cup extra-virgin olive oil

1. Bring a small saucepan of water to a boil. Add the basil leaves, if using; blanch 10 seconds. Drain the leaves, then transfer immediately to a bowl of ice water. Remove the basil from the ice water immediately. Blot the leaves dry with paper towels; cut into thin strips. Set aside.

2. In a blender or food processor, process the lemon juice, mustard, red onion, garlic, salt, pepper, and sugar until blended, about 1 minute. With the machine running, gradually add the grapeseed and olive oils in a thin, steady stream through the feed tube, and process until the vinaigrette is smooth and emulsified. Add the basil, if using, pulsing just until blended.

Makes 3½ cups

LENTIL SALAD

This salad encompasses a variety of textures and flavors and is a healthful side to lunch or dinner. French lentils cook quickly and have a creamy interior and a sturdy texture.

---

1 cup French green lentils, picked over and rinsed	1½ tablespoons walnut oil
2 cups cold water	1 tablespoon sherry vinegar
1 bay leaf	1 tablespoon chopped flat-leaf parsley
¾ teaspoon turmeric	1½ teaspoons Dijon mustard
½ cinnamon stick	1½ teaspoons kosher salt
2 tablespoons extra-virgin olive oil	¾ teaspoon fresh thyme leaves
¼ cup finely diced carrot	¼ teaspoon freshly ground black pepper
¼ cup finely diced Spanish onion	⅔ cup toasted walnuts (see "Toasting Nuts," page 137)
1½ teaspoons minced garlic	

1. In a large pot, combine the lentils, water, bay leaf, turmeric, and cinnamon stick. Bring to a boil. Reduce the heat and cook the lentils until tender to the bite, 20 to 25 minutes. Drain and cool slightly. Remove the bay leaf and cinnamon stick.

2. Meanwhile, in a small sauté pan, heat the olive oil over medium–high heat. Add the carrot, onion, and garlic; cook, stirring, 2 minutes. Set aside.

3. In a large bowl, whisk together the walnut oil, vinegar, parsley, mustard, salt, thyme, and pepper. Add the lentils and sautéed vegetables; stir to coat with the dressing. Stir in the walnuts.

Makes 4 cups

BLACK BEAN SALAD

Each of the ingredients in this salad adds to its distinct flavor. In particular, the lime juice is tart, the cilantro provides a fresh pungency, and the rice wine vinegar lends a subtle sweetness.

1 cup dried black beans, picked over and rinsed

6 cups cold water

½ teaspoon ground cumin

½ teaspoon chili powder

½ teaspoon paprika

¼ teaspoon turmeric

½ cup diced red bell pepper

1 green onion, sliced into ¼"-thick rounds

1 jalapeño chile pepper, seeded and minced

¼ cup fresh lime juice

¼ cup chopped fresh cilantro

2 cloves garlic, minced

1 tablespoon soy sauce

2 teaspoons red wine vinegar

2 teaspoons rice wine vinegar

½ teaspoon freshly ground black pepper

¼ teaspoon kosher salt

½ cup extra-virgin olive oil

1. Combine the beans and water in a large saucepan; cover and let the beans soak overnight.

2. Bring the soaked beans and the water to a boil. Reduce the heat, cover, and cook until the beans are tender, 35 to 40 minutes. Drain the beans in a colander; transfer to a large bowl.

3. In a small sauté pan, toast the cumin, chili powder, paprika, and turmeric over low heat until fragrant, about 1 minute. Add to the beans. Stir in the bell pepper, green onion, and jalapeño.

4. In a medium bowl, whisk together the lime juice, cilantro, garlic, soy sauce, vinegars, black pepper, and salt until blended. Whisk in the olive oil. Pour the vinaigrette over the beans; toss well to coat.

Makes 3 cups

ROASTED CORN SALAD

Roasting corn heightens its natural sweetness, while the ricotta salata (a firmer, more aged version of creamy ricotta) adds texture to this salad. With perfectly ripe tomatoes and a simple dressing of vinegar and extra-virgin olive oil, this salad is a completely satisfying lunch on a hot summer day.

4   ears yellow corn, shucked

2   tablespoons extra-virgin olive oil

Juice of ½ lemon

1   tablespoon rice wine vinegar

1   tablespoon minced garlic

1   teaspoon kosher salt

½   teaspoon freshly ground black pepper

1   plum tomato, seeded and diced

¾   cup diced ricotta salata

½   cup finely diced red bell pepper

1   green onion, thinly sliced

1. Preheat the oven to 400°F. Cut the bottom and top ends of each corn cob. Stand 1 ear of corn on its end on a cutting board, holding the ear near the top. With a large knife parallel to the cob, cut the kernels off. Repeat with the remaining corn. Place the kernels on a baking tray and drizzle with 1 tablespoon of the oil. Roast about 15 minutes or until the corn starts to turn golden. Set aside to cool.

2. In a large bowl, whisk together the remaining 1 tablespoon oil, lemon juice, vinegar, garlic, salt, and black pepper. Add the corn, tomato, ricotta, bell pepper, and green onion; toss to combine.

Makes 3 cups

RESOURCES

Ingredient Sources

The Baker's Catalogue (King Arthur Flour)
P.O. Box 876
Norwich, VT 05055-0876
(800) 827-6836
www.bakerscatalogue.com
www.kingarthurflour.com
Bread flour, whole wheat flour, rye flour; ba-
nettons and other baking tools; crystal sugar

Boyajian Inc.
349 Lenox Street
Norwood, MA 02062
(800) 419-4677
www.boyajianinc.com
Pure orange oil, lemon oil, lime oil, and
other flavored oils

Caviar Assouline
505 Vine Street
Philadelphia, PA 19106
(800) 521-4491
www.caviarassouline.com
Olives, chocolates, De Zaan Special Black
Cocoa, crystal sugar

Cherry Central Inc.
P.O. Box 988
Traverse City, MI 49685
(231) 946-1860
www.cherrycentral.com
Dried berries

Good Food Inc.
4960 Horseshoe Pike
P.O. Box 160
Honey Brook, PA 19344
(800) 327-4406
Fax: (610) 273-7652
www.goldenbarrel.com
Grade B maple syrup

Nielsen-Massey Vanillas
1550 Shields Drive
Waukegan, IL 60085-8307
(800) 525-PURE
Fax: (847) 578-1570
www.nielsenmassey.com
Tahitian and Madagascar vanilla beans;
pure vanilla extract

Premier Malt
25760 Groesbeck Highway, Suite 103
Warren, MI 48089
(800) 521-1057
Malt extract

Shelburne Farms
Shelburne, VT 05482
(802) 985-8686
Vermont Cheddar cheese, maple syrup

12th Street Cantina
12th and Arch Streets (Reading Terminal Market)
Philadelphia, PA 19107
(215) 625-0321
Mexican ground cinnamon

Williams-Sonoma
200 South Broad Street, #M6
Philadelphia, PA 19102
(877) 812-6235
www.williamssonoma.com
Dried lavender leaves

Baking Equipment

Fante's Kitchen Wares Shop
1006 S. Ninth Street
Philadelphia, PA 19147-4798
(800) 44-fante
www.fantes.com
Cake pans, flan rings, molds, and basic equipment; baking ingredients

F.B.M. Baking Machines
Cranbury, NJ 08512
(800) 449-0433
Proofing couches, baskets, and professional ovens

Foster's Gourmet Cookware
12th and Arch Streets (Reading Terminal Market)
Philadelphia, PA 19107
(800) 734-8511
www.fosterscookware.com
General baking equipment; pans and molds

Previn Inc.
2044 Rittenhouse Square
Philadelphia, PA 19103
(215) 985-1996
www.previninc.com
Cannele molds, tart pans, and professional baking tools and equipment

Williams-Sonoma
200 South Broad Street, #M6
Philadelphia, PA 19102
(877) 812-6235
www.williamssonoma.com
Basic equipment; baking ingredients

Linens and Tableware

Monique Messin Shop
1742 Sansom Street
Philadelphia PA 19103
(215) 557-1060

Miscellaneous

Chloe
232 Arch Street
Philadelphia, PA 19106
(215) 629-2337

Picnic
Shops at the Left Bank
3131 Walnut Street
Philadelphia, PA 19104
(215) 222-1608

White Dog Café
3420 Sansom Street
Philadelphia, PA 19103
(215) 386-9224

EQUIPMENT

Being equipped with the right tool for the right job makes life easier. Here is a list of tools that are useful for the recipes in this book.

Baking Sheets

Heavy-duty metal baking trays (13" × 18") are standard and will fit into most home ovens. They can be found at any good kitchenware store.

Baking Stone

Baking stones are more commonly referred to as pizza stones and are most often found in a round shape. A square, unglazed quarry tile cut to fit the entire surface of the middle rack of your oven works best and enables you to bake two loaves at a time. Baking stones are always preheated with the oven. They provide a more intense, even bottom heat that helps to create a thin, crackling crust.

Baskets for Rising

(bannetons, cloth-lined bannetons, baker's canvas)
Couches and bannetons are used to support rising loaves and to impart a decorative pattern on the final loaves. If you're using a banneton, it is important to use the proper size in relation to the loaf size. We prefer to use white rye flour for proofing baskets and canvas because it prevents sticking and at the same time helps the rising loaves retain their moisture.

Bench Knives, Scrapers, and Spatulas

These are useful tools for blending ingredients and cleaning bowls and work surfaces. Long-handled heat-resistant spatulas are useful for cooking custards.

Cake Pans

Cake pans come in various sizes and shapes. Choose a standard 8" and 9" round for the recipes in this book. Then experiment with individual cake pans or other fancifully designed pans. Nonstick pans are a great investment.

Food Processor

Even if your knife skills are good, a processor is very helpful. It can mix a pesto or mayonnaise in seconds.

KitchenAid Heavy-Duty Electric Mixer

(attachments: dough hook, paddle)

A heavy-duty electric mixer is helpful for properly kneading extremely wet or very firm bread doughs, which are more difficult to mix and knead by hand. This is definitely a worthwhile investment if you become a bread-making enthusiast. Also great for mixing cookie doughs and cake and muffin batters.

Lame

A 3"-long stainless steel rod to which a double-edge razor is attached. It is used to score the surface of loaves. A sharp serrated knife may be substituted.

Measuring Cups and Spoons

A set of graduated measuring cups and spoons is helpful for measuring amounts of flour, sugar, and salt. Be sure to level the tops with the back of a knife for accuracy.

Parchment Paper

Useful for lining baking trays for cookies and breads. It prevents sticking and saves on cleanups.

Spray Bottle

Label and dedicate a spray bottle for creating steam in your oven. Be sure it is only used for water.

Rolling Pin

The type of rolling pin one uses (either a standard ball-bearing pin with handles or a French pin without handles) is a matter of personal preference. Our preference is the pin with handles for rolling out pastry doughs.

Tart Pans

Bottomless flan rings for individual 4" tarts or larger 10" tarts will give a professional look. In this case the baking tray becomes the tart pan bottom. If you prefer, fluted pans with removable bottoms may be easier to use. Rectangular pans also make a beautiful presentation.

Thermometers

It is useful to have three types of thermometers. A long-stemmed, instant-read cooking thermometer is good to check dough and ingredient temperatures. A room thermometer will help you to adjust water temperature when mixing bread doughs. Also, an oven thermometer will let you know what temperature your oven is—pretty much all ovens have inaccuracies.

INDEX

Conversion Chart

These equivalents have been slightly rounded to make measuring easier.

Volume Measurements

U.S.	Imperial	Metric
¼ tsp	–	1 ml
½ tsp	–	2 ml
1 tsp	–	5 ml
1 Tbsp	–	15 ml
2 Tbsp (1 oz)	1 fl oz	30 ml
¼ cup (2 oz)	2 fl oz	60 ml
⅓ cup (3 oz)	3 fl oz	80 ml
½ cup (4 oz)	4 fl oz	120 ml
⅔ cup (5 oz)	5 fl oz	160 ml
¾ cup (6 oz)	6 fl oz	180 ml
1 cup (8 oz)	8 fl oz	240 ml

Weight Measurements

U.S.	Metric
1 oz	30 g
2 oz	60 g
4 oz (¼ lb)	115 g
5 oz (⅓ lb)	145 g
6 oz	170 g
7 oz	200 g
8 oz (½ lb)	230 g
10 oz	285 g
12 oz (¾ lb)	340 g
14 oz	400 g
16 oz (1 lb)	455 g
2.2 lb	1 kg

Length Measurements

U.S.	Metric
¼"	0.6 cm
½"	1.25 cm
1"	2.5 cm
2"	5 cm
4"	11 cm
6"	15 cm
8"	20 cm
10"	25 cm
12" (1')	30 cm

Pan Sizes

U.S.	Metric
8" cake pan	20 × 4 cm sandwich or cake tin
9" cake pan	23 × 3.5 cm sandwich or cake tin
11" × 7" baking pan	28 × 18 cm baking tin
13" × 9" baking pan	32.5 × 23 cm baking tin
15" × 10" baking pan	38 × 25.5 cm baking tin (Swiss roll tin)
1½ qt baking dish	1.5 liter baking dish
2 qt baking dish	2 liter baking dish
2 qt rectangular baking dish	30 × 19 cm baking dish
9" pie plate	22 × 4 or 23 × 4 cm pie plate
7" or 8" springform pan	18 or 20 cm springform or loose-bottom cake tin
9" × 5" loaf pan	23 × 13 cm or 2 lb narrow loaf tin or pâté tin

Temperatures

Fahrenheit	Centigrade	Gas
140°	60°	–
160°	70°	–
180°	80°	–
225°	105°	¼
250°	120°	½
275°	135°	1
300°	150°	2
325°	160°	3
350°	180°	4
375°	190°	5
400°	200°	6
425°	220°	7
450°	230°	8
475°	245°	9
500°	260°	–